How to deter

How to Determine Author and Title Entries According to AACR

An Interpretive Guide with Card Examples

by

Donald J. Lehnus

1971

OCEANA PUBLICATIONS, INC.
Dobbs Ferry, New York

PREFACE

The new cataloging code represents a great step forward in improving certain catalog entries as well as advancing the standardization of international cataloging practices, and all catalogers should be aware of the progress made by the new code. The principal objective of this manual is to explain these new rules for the novice cataloger. Also, at the same time the author hopes to produce a useful guide by pointing out to those experienced catalogers who wish to keep abreast of current practices the principal variations between the ALA Cataloging Rules for Author and Title Entries and the Anglo-American Cataloging Rules. For those persons especially interested in the standardization and improvement of cataloging practices in the future several major differences between the North American and the British texts have been brought out and contrasted.

For a better understanding of the rules it is first necessary to have in mind the general arrangement of the new code. It is divided into three main parts: the first part includes the rules for (a) determination of personal, corporate and title entries, (b) the proper manner in which entries are written, and (c) references; the second part covers descriptive cataloging; and the third part contains special rules for non-book materials which supplement rules from the other two parts of the code.

This guide treats only rules of Part I, and is not a comprehensive treatment of all rules contained therein. Excluded are the rules for certain legal and religious publications, rules 20-32, those for religious bodies and officials, rules 92-96, and rule 123 for special headings for legal publications. Other exclusions are those rules or parts of rules which are either so brief that any additional comment would be redundant or those already having such a clear explanation and excellent examples that no further explanation is needed.

The explanations and examples given in this publication are intended only as supplementary material to be used directly in conjunction with the full text of the Anglo-American Cataloging Rules.

The arrangement of Part I is a very logical one for using the code in actual practice, but to introduce cataloging to the beginner the rules are not treated here in their numerical order. The five chapters of Part I of the Anglo-American Cataloging Rules are set up thusly: Chapter 1 contains the rules for determing main and secondary entries. Once the entries have been decided upon the next procedure is to find out the correct form of a name and the proper way in which it should appear as a heading. For personal names one refers to Chapter 2 and for names of corporate bodies it is Chapter 3 that is needed. Chapter 4 and 5 are applicable to both personal and corporate names. Chapter 4 introduces a whole new concept of using uniform titles in the cataloging of subjects other than music, and Chapter 5 serves as a guide for making reference cards.

The arrangement of the material in this work is made on the assumption that after having established a firm base at the very beginning one should always begin with the simple and most ordinary and work toward the difficult and least common. Therefore the first section deals with the proper form of a personal name and how to write it as a heading; proceeding then to the rules which indicate how to choose which name to use as a main entry and which ones for secondary entries. From that point the order is one that progresses in what has been found the most practical way to teach these rules, based on actual classroom experience in teaching the new code since its publication in 1967.

Throughout the text the ALA Cataloging Rules for Author and Title Entries and the Anglo-American Cataloging Rules are referred to respectively as the "ALA rules" and the "AA rules".

TABLE OF CONTENTS

CHAPTER I

PERSONAL NAMES -- Rules 40-53

A very basic aspect of cataloging is the correct form used for personal names. The main entries most often used are those involving names of individuals, and for this reason it is important that this be discussed first.

40. Basic rule.

This basic rule for personal names now makes it correct to do what many libraries have been doing for years, and that is, using the form of a name as it is generally known to the public. A pseudonym, a single forename without a surname, a nickname, an anglicized form of a foreign name, any form of a name albeit incomplete, or any other word or phrase by which a person is best known is the correct way to list a person in the catalog. However, there is no provision for the use of initials alone as a heading. In fact, throughout the AA rules headings that might begin with initials are consistently avoided wherever possible.

Advocating the use of a form of a name by which a person is commonly identified is a radical change from previous practice. The ALA rules stated that the name should be in the vernacular and that the form chosen should be the most authentic. However, the same ALA rule states that a less authentic name can be used in those instances where the most authentic form has been little used and another form has been used predominantly by the person concerned as well as in reference sources. But, unfortunately in actual practice the emphasis was placed on using the most authentic form without regard to the best known form.

It should be noted here that the form of a name determined for any person is always used without variation whenever it occurs as a heading, whether as a main or secondary entry, or as a subject heading.

CHOICE AND FORM OF NAME.

Rules 41 through 45 illustrate different cases where problems arise for catalogers trying to determine the best form of a name to use for certain individuals. In all too many cases a person can be known by different names or variations on one name. In any one given case this may be due to one or more factors such as the use of pseudonyms, marriage, acquisition of a title, inconsistent use of forenames and/or initials, different translitera- tions of names not written in the Roman alphabet, con- fusion in distinguishing forenames and surnames, and vari- ations in spelling. The purpose of these rules is to guide catalogers to make the correct choice and hopefully all will choose the same form of name for any given person.

41. Choice among different names -- General rule.

This is the general rule for the following section on choice and form of name and lists three factors in order of preference which should be used in determining which form of the name to use. These three factors are: (a) the name by which he is generally identified in ref- erence sources, (b) the name by which he is most frequently identified in his works, and (c) the latest name he has used.

42. Pseudonyms.

42-A. Many authors choose to use a pseudonym instead of their real names and this is done for a variety of reasons. Publishers respect this privilege of authors to use "noms de plume" and the public will know a work by the name that appears on the title page. This part of the rule indicates that if an author has used only one pseudonym for all his writings and is better known by this rather than by his real name, then the entry should be under the pseudonym. This includes pseudonyms which consist of only a single forename, a surname, or combination thereof. A pseudonym is treated in the same

manner as any other name. No indication is made to show
that it is not a real name as was done previously according to the ALA rules. This practical innovation advocates
the use of a heading such as: "Caballero, Fernán, 1796-
1877" instead of the cumbersome and overly long one previously used for that author which was: "Caballero,
Fernán, pseud. of Cecilia Böhl de Faber, 1796-1877".
Dates of a person's birth and death are added or eliminated
for the same reasons as they would be for a real name
(cf. rule 52).

Twain, Mark, 1835-1910.
    Tom Sawyer abroad, and Tom Sawyer,
detective. Illustrated by Gerald
McCann. New York, Collier Books /1962/
    224p. illus.

Card 1

X, Dr. Jacobus.
    The basis of passional psychology; a study
of the laws of love in man and the lower animals,
by Dr. Jacobus X.   New York, American
Anthropological Society [19--]
    396 p. 24 cm.

Card 2

Thomas, Lately,
    A debonair scoundrel; an episode in the moral history of
San Francisco. [1st ed.] New York, Holt, Rinehart and
Winston [1962]

    422 p. illus. 22 cm.

    Includes bibliography.

Card 3

    1. Ruef, Abraham, 1864-1936. 2. Corruption (in politics)—San
Francisco. 3. San Francisco—Pol. & govt.   I. Title.

JS1449.T47   364.13   62-12137 ‡

Library of Congress   [5]

```
     Edwina, 1893-
        Sinbad again!  New York, Coward-
     McCann, 1932.
        3p.  /86/p. of illus.                        Card 4
```

```
     Seuss, Dr., 1904-
        The Sneetches, and other stories.
     Written and illustrated by Dr. Seuss.
     New York, Random House, c1960.
        65p.  illus.

                                                       Card 5
```

42-B.   This part of the rule deals with those authors who
have used two or more pseudonyms, or have used their real
names for some writings and one or more pseudonyms for
other works. It is stated that in these cases of two or
more names the name chosen should be the one which is usually found on the title pages of modern editions as well
as the name under which the individual is found in reference works. In case of doubt, prefer the real name.

        This is one of the few cases in the AA rules where
an alternative rule is given, and it is what should be
followed. The alternative rule permits the cataloger to
use whatever name appears on the title page of that particular work as the heading. It is suggested that there be
reference cards in the catalog to connect the various
names.

The examples given under 42-B illustrate how advantageous it would be to prefer the alternative and give the cataloger the choice of using several names for a person or placing all writings under a single name depending on how the person was best known. The use of Charlotte Bronte instead of Currer Bell would be preferred because Charlotte Bronte is the name used in modern editions of her works, in reference sources and this is how she is best known. But, on the other hand there would be no real advantage in using a single heading for all the writings of Isaac Asimov or Pearl Buck. These two authors have used their real names for a certain type of writing and pseudonyms for other kinds of writings. References to connect the various names of the same person would be the best way to handle such authors as John Creasey, Isaac Asimov and Pearl Buck.

French, Paul, 1920–
    Lucky Star and the rings of Saturn.
Garden City, N.Y., Doubleday, 1958.
    179p.

Card 6

French, Paul, 1920–

    see also his real name:

Asimov, Isaac, 1920–

Card 7

Asimov, Isaac, 1920–
    Life and energy. Garden City, N.Y.,
Doubleday, 1962.
    380p. illus.

Card 8

```
Asimov, Isaac, 1920-

    see also his pseudonym:

French, Paul, 1920-                          Card 9
```

43. Fullness.

     Very often an author's name will appear in various
degrees of fullness in different works and/or in the variety of editions of a work. The purpose of this rule is to
point out to the cataloger the factors which will help
determine the fullness of the name needed in each individual case. The extent of fullness depends on the fullest
form which has appeared in a prominent position in an
author's works and adding to this if necessary to distinguish it from other similar names.

44. Language.

44-A. Names in the Roman alphabet.

     When a name is found written in several languages,
preference should be given to the form that has become
most firmly established in reference sources and if no one
definite form can be determined there are four guides to
help determine which would be the best form. However, it
is pointed out that when an English form of a name exists
and is in common usage then this is the form that definitely must be used. The ALA rules preferred Latin and
vernacular forms in any cases even when there were established English forms.

Fournival, Richard de, *fl.* 1246–1260.
La biblionomia de Richard de Fournival du manuscrit
636 de la Bibliothèque de la Sorbonne. Texte en facsimilé
avec la transcription de Léopold Delisle ₍par₎ H. J. de
Vleeschauwer. Pretoria, 1965.

₍79₎ 1. 25 cm. (Mousaion ; livres et bibliothèques, 62)

John IV, King of Portugal, 1604-1656.
Cartas de el-rei d. Joao IV para
diversas autoridades do reino, publi-
cadas e prefaciadas pelo académico
titular fundador, P.M. Laranjo Coehlo.
Lisboa /Editorial Atica7 1940.
xiii, 587p.

Juvenal.
Satires. Translated by Rolfe
Humphries. Bloomington, Indiana
University Press, 1958.
186p.

Viperanus, Joannes Antonius, *d.* 1610.
De poetica libri tres. Antverpiae, Ex officina C. Plantini,
architypographi regij, 1579.

155 p. 18 cm.

Virgil.
The Aeneid. Translated by C.
Day Lewis. Garden City, N.Y.,
Doubleday, 1953.
320p.

44-B.   Names not in the Roman alphabet.

There are names from many parts of the world which are written in other alphabets or in characters and must be romanized, i.e. transliterated into the Roman alphabet. Transliterations attempt to rewrite words so that they can be read and pronounced in the same way as in the original form.   For this reason words will be transliterated differently into the various languages which use the same alphabet, e.g.   The Russian word, "COBET", is transliterated into English as "Soviet", but into German as "Sowjet". Both attempt to approximate the original sound, but are written differently so that those who do not speak the same language can read it the same as it is pronounced in Russian.

Transliterations are further complicated by the fact that there are several systems in use to transliterate from one alphabet into a single language using another alphabet.

This rule establishes guidelines to follow in those cases where a variety of transliterations exist for the same name.

The alternative given for rule 44-B is the most practical for the majority of libraries.   This alternative advocates that the transliterated form found most frequently in the English language translations and reference sources in English should be used in any library that considers these forms to be better suited to the needs of its users.

```
Cavafy, Constantine P., 1863-1933.
   Poems.   Translated into English
with a few notes by John Mavrogordato.
With an introduction by Rex Warner.               Card
New York, Grove Press, 1952.                        15
   199p.
```

Chekhov, Anton Pavlovich, 1860-1904.
    The boor, a comedy in one act,
by Anton Tchekoff. Translated by
Hilmar Baukhage. New York, S. French
/1915/
        20p.

Card
16

Mishima, Yukio.
    The sound of waves. Translated
by Meredith Weatherby. Drawings by
Yoshinori Kinoshita. New York,
Knopf, 1956.
        182p. illus.

Card
17

Omar Khayyam.
    Rubaiyat. Translated by Edward
Fitzgerald. Introduction by Thomas
Yoseloff. New York, Fine Editions
Press /1957/
        258p.

Card
18

Sun, Yat-sen, 1866-1925.
    The international development of
China. Taipei, China Cultural Service
/1953/
        233p. illus.

Card
19

Tolstoy, Leo, graf, 1828-1910.
    The long exile, and other stories
for children, by Count Lyof N. Tolstoi.
Translated from the Russian by Nathan
Haskell Dole. New York, Crowell /c1888/
        vi, 363p.

Card
20

45. Spelling.

45-A.   Whenever there are variant spellings of a person's
name the one most commonly found in his works or in reference sources should be preferred.

Lindsay, Sir David, fl.1440-1555.
  /Poems/
  The poetical works of Sir David
Lyndsay. With memoir, notes and
glossary by David Laing. Edinburgh,
Paterson, 1879.
  3v. illus.

Card
21

45-C.   When hyphens are found between forenames they
should always be retained when they are used through personal preference. Excepted from this are French forenames in which the hyphens should always be omitted.

Wu, Wen-tsun.
    A theory of imbedding, immersion and
isotopy in a Euclidean space.   Peking, Science
Press, 1965.
    xv, 291 p. 23 cm.

Card
22

Dubois, Jean Baptiste, b.1778-
    Marton et Frontin; ou Assault
de valets, comedie en un acte, en
prose, par Jean-Baptiste Dubois.
Paris, Barba, 1815.
    23p.

Card
23

ENTRY OF NAME.

Rules 46 through 51 indicate the various manners in which names and titles are written so that they may be alphabetized by the proper element of the name.

46. Entry under surname.

This is a very basic rule to guide the cataloger in choosing the element or elements of the name that compose the surname and writing them in the proper manner.

46-A. Last element as a surname.

Fortunately the majority of works cataloged in most libraries are written by persons with one or two given names and a surname, for which the entry is made by just simply inverting the name so that the surname is the first element and then followed by a comma and the given names. But, not all names are this simple and the cataloger must be able to recognize those names which can not be treated in this manner.

Asheim, Lester Eugene, 1914–
    La preparación de los bibliotecarios en los Estados Unidos de América, por Lester E. Asheim. Washington, Unión Panamericana, 1964.

Card 24

Bloomfield, Barry Cambray.
    Theses on Asia; accepted by universities in the United Kingdom and Ireland, 1877–1964; compiled by B. C. Bloomfield. London, Cass, 1967.

    xi, 127 p. table. 25½ cm. 63/–

(B 67-20411)

Card 25

Powell, Lawrence Clark, 1906–
    Fortune & friendship, an autobiography. New York, R. R. Bowker Co., 1968.

    xiii, 227 p. ports. 23 cm.

Card 26

    I. Title.

Z720.P65   027.7′0924 (B)   67–29798

Library of Congress   [5]

46-B. Compound surnames.

There are various types of compound surnames and
the form used in cataloging should be determined by the
way the writer prefers to have his name written. If this
form is not known then the name should be searched in reference sources and the most predominantly found form
should be the one used. Hyphenated surnames cause no problems as it is obvious that the two elements belong together.
In other cases where there is no indication that two elements form a single surname, reference sources must be
searched to determine if it is a compound surname. Of
course, before such a search is made the cataloger would
have to have a specific reason to bother to look up the
name, because in all too many cases it would not be obvious
that it was a compound surname. In these cases it would be
entered incorrectly, but mistakes can always be corrected
later and at a much more economical rate than checking each
and every name just to see if it is compound. All persons
with compound names should be urged to join the two elements
with a hyphen.

Bright-Paul, Anthony.
　　　Stairway to Subud.　New York, Dharma
Book Co. [1965]
　　　256 p. 18 cm.

Card
27

Badstübner-Gröger, Sibylle.
　　Bibliographie zur Kunstgeschichte von Berlin und Pots-
dam. Berlin, Akademie-Verlag, 1968.
　　　xiii, 320 p. 28 cm. (Schriften zur Kunstgeschichte, Heft 13)
DM 60.-
　　　　　　　　　　　　　　　(GDB 68-A53-312)

Card
28

Ben-Amos, Paula.
　　Bibliography of Benin art. New York, Library, Museum
of Primitive Art, 1968.
　　　17 p. 28 cm. (Primitive art bibliographies, no. 6)
　　Cover title.

　　1. Art--Benin, Nigeria (Province)--Bibl.　I. Title. II. Title:
Benin art.　(Series)

Z5961.N6B4　　　　　016.709'669'2　　　68-6989

Library of Congress　　　[2]

Card
29

Florén Lozano, Luis, 1913–
　　Obras de referencia y generales de la bibliografía colombiana. Medellín, Editorial Universidad de Antioquia, 1968.
　　204, 22 l.　28 cm.　(Publicaciones de la E. I. B.　Serie: Bibliografía no. 28)　200.00
　　　　　　　　　　　　　　　　　　　　LACAP 68-7095

Card
30

Lange-Hansen, Preben, 1924–
　　The carrying capacity of curved beams;
tests with curved beams of steel loaded in the
beam plane.　Kobenhavn, 1956.
　　13 p.　illus., diagrs. 26 cm.　(Den Polytekniske laereanstalt, Copenhagen.　Laboratoriet
for bygningsteknik.　Meddelelse. nr. 6)

Card
31

Lone Dog, Louise.
　　Strange journey, the vision life of a psychic
Indian woman.　Ed. by Vinson Brown; illus. by
Tso Yazzy (Chester Kahn) Navajo.　Healdsburg,
Calif., Naturegraph Publishers, c1964.
　　68 p.　illus. (part. col.) 22 cm.

Card
32

Touchard-Lafosse, Georges, 1780-1847.
　　Chroniques de l'OEil-de-Boeuf, des petits
appartements de la cour et des salons de Paris
sous le règne de Louis XIII [par] G. Touchard-
Lafosse.　Éd. établi et présentée par Hubert
Juin.　[Paris] Le Livre club du libraire [1965]
　　347 p.　illus. (Le Livre club du libraire, 187)

Card
33

Vesey FitzGerald, Brian Seymour, 1900–
　　Town fox, country fox.　[London]
A. Deutsch [1965]
　　160 p.　illus. 22 cm. (A Survival book, 4)
　　1. Foxes.　I. Title.　(Series)
NIC　　　　　　　　　　　　NUC67-1464

Card
34

46-B-3-b. Married women.

The form called for here differs from that of the
ALA rules which stated that the maiden name was to be enclosed in parentheses and always used in the heading when
known. The use of the maiden name is now restricted just
to those persons who continue to use it as a part of their
names, and it is never enclosed in parentheses. The form
of the name should be established according to rules 40
and 41. Attention should be called to the fact that Czech,
Hungarian, Italian, Spanish and Spanish-American women
always retain their maiden names to which is added the
husband's surname to form a compound surname of which the
first element is the maiden name.

Lindbergh, Anne Morrow, 1906– 　　Gift from the sea. New York, Vintage Books /1966, c1955/ 　　127p. illus.	Card 35

Otero Revilla de Martinez, Flora. 　　Devocionario, poemas. ₁1. ed.　　Puebla, México, Impr. Estrada, 1962₁ 　　159 p. illus. 20 cm. (Publicaciones del grupo literario Bohemia Poblana)	Card 36

Ridler, Anne Bradby, 1912–
　　Selected poems. New York, Macmillan, 1961.
　　96 p. 22 cm.

　　　　　　　　　　　　　　　　Full name: Anne Barbara Bradby Ridler.

PR6035.I 54A17 1961　　　　821.912　　　　61–11095 ↕

Library of Congress　　　　₁10₁

Card
37

46-D.   Words indicating relationship following surnames.

The words Junior, Filho, Neto and Sobrinho are
added to Brazilian and Portuguese surnames to form a compound surname with this as the second element. This is
consistent with current usage in Brazil and Portugal and
is a change from the practice of disregarding these terms
as was done according to the ALA rules. It should be
noted that the addition of the word Junior to the surname
is not normally done for other nationalities as illustrated in the examples of rule 53.

```
Rodrigues Junior, Manuel.
        Moçambique; terra de Portugal.    Lisboa,
Agência Geral do Ultramar, 1965.
        284 p.  23 cm.

                                              Card
                                              38
```

46-E.   Surnames with separately written prefixes.

46-E-1.   Articles and prepositions.

Many surnames include a separately written prefix,
which consist of an article, a preposition, or a combination of the two. The use of these as part of the surname
varies according to the nationality of the individual.
The manner in which these are written changes from country
to country, and even though the same name may be used in
several countries the form used in cataloging will depend
on the practice followed in the language of the individual
and not on the practice in the country where the surname
originated. The following examples show various types of
prefixes and how they should be treated according to the
nationality of the individual.

American and English.
        Enter under the prefix.

De Mille, Cecil Blount, 1881–1959.
        Autobiography. Edited by Donald Hayne. Englewood
Cliffs, N. J., Prentice-Hall [1959]

465 p. illus. 24 cm.

Card
39

DeWeerd, Harvey Arthur, 1902–
        President Wilson fights his war; World War I and the
American intervention, by Harvey A. DeWeerd. New York,
Macmillan [1968]

xxi, 457 p. illus., maps. 24 cm. (The Wars of the United States)

Card
40

Di Bella, Carlos Arthur Williston, 1940–
        Nonlinear programming in chemical plant
design.   [n. p.] 1966.
        1 v.

Card
41

Dos Passos, Cyril Franklin.
        Bad money drives out good.   [Mendham,
N. J., 1965]
        4 p. 23 cm.

Card
42

Le Masurier, John, 1917–
        Field events.   [Harmondsworth, Eng.;
Baltimore] Penguin Books [1964]
        127 p. illus., ports. 19 cm. (Improve your
athletics, v. 2)

Card
43

L'Engle, Madeleine.
        The love letters. New York, Farrar, Straus and Giroux
[1966]

365 p. 22 cm.

Card
44

I. Title.

PZ3.L54646Lo

66–20170

Library of Congress   [3]

American and English.

TenBroek, Jacobus.
California's dual system of family law: its
origin, development, and present status.
[n. p.] 1965.
1 v. (various pagings)
Bibliographical footnotes.

Card
45

Ter Laan, Hans, *ed.*
Russian literary gems. Литературные отрывки. From
the works of Derzhavin [and others] New York, R. D. Cortina Co., 1962.
63 p. 24 cm. (Cortina classics series)

Card
46

Van der Plank, J   E
Disease resistance in plants [by] J. E. Van der Plank.
New York, Academic Press, 1968.
x, 206 p. illus. 24 cm.

Card
47

Vandervelde, Conrad, 1879-
Hollanders in Kansas.   Emporia, Kansas
State Teachers College, Dept. of English, 1963.
24 p. illus. (Heritage of Kansas, v. 7,

Card
48

Van Dyke, Charles Hillis.
A study of the properties of the silicon-
silicon bond in disilanyl compounds.
[Philadelphia] 1964.
xxvi, 230 l. diagrs., tables. 29 cm.

Card
49

Van Roy, Edward, 1937-
Economic frontiers: a study of economies in
the hills of North Thailand.   Austin, Tex.,
1965 [c1966]
219, [1] l. illus., maps, tables. 28 cm.
Thesis (Ph. D.)-University of Texas, 1965.
Vita.
Bibliography: l. 210-219.
1. Thailand—Economic policy. 2. Thailand—
Econ. condit. 3. Economic development.
I. Title.
TxU   NUC67-1431

Card
50

Dutch and Flemish.

Enter under the part of the name following the prefix, except if the prefix is "ver", in which case
it is entered under the prefix.

Bosch, Hendrik van den, 1938-
    Lysolecithins, their enzymatic formation and
conversions.   Utrecht, 1966.
    72 p. illus. 24 cm.

Card
51

Daal, H   J   van.
    Mobility of charge carriers in silicon car-
bide. [Eindhoven, Philips' Gloeilampen-
fabrieken, 1965]
    92 p. illus. 24 cm. (Philips research
reports. Supplements, 1965, no. 3)

Card
52

Gogh, Vincent van, 1853–1890.
    Letters to Émile Bernard, edited, translated and with a
foreword by Douglas Lord.   New York, Museum of
Modern Art, 1938.

    xi, 124 p. 32 pl. (incl. front., ports., facsims.) 28½ x 22ᶜᵐ.

Card
53

Hooch, Pieter de, *17th cent.*
    Pieter de Hooch; the master's paintings in 180 reproduc-
tions, with an appendix on the genre painters in the manner
of Pieter de Hooch and Hendrik van der Burch's art. Published with an introduction by Wilhelm R. Valentiner. London, A. Zwemmer [1930]
    xlvii, [2], 305, [1] p. incl. plates, ports. 26ᶜᵐ.
Printed in Germany.

Card
54

Sluis, P   A   van der.
    Cultuurtechnische ontwikkelingen in de Friese
Wouden na 1918.   Drachten, Laverman, 1963.
      100 p. illus. (Wâldrige nr, 12)
      1. Land—Friesland. 2. Friesland—Descr.
  MH DLC   NUC66-90242

Card
55

French.

If the prefix consists of an article or of a contraction of an article and a preposition, enter under the prefix.

Des Cars, Guy
Les filles de joie, roman. Paris,
Flammarion /1959/
284p.

Card 56

Du Bouchet, André
Au deuxième étage. Lithographies de
J. Hélion. Paris, Editions du Dragon,
1956.
64p. illus.

Card 57

La Bonnardière, Anne Marie.
Chrétiennes des premiers siecles.
Paris, Editions Ouvrières /1957/
155p.

Card 58

Le Bihan, Alexis.
Illustration de la langue bretonne; exposition du 26 mars au 2 juin 1958. [Par M. Le Bihan. Rennes, 1958]

58 p. 21 cm.

Card 59

Le Grand, Yves, 1908–
Light, colour and vision; approved translation [from the French] by R. W. G. Hunt, J. W. T. Walsh and F. R. W. Hunt. English 2nd ed. London, Chapman & Hall, 1968.

xiii, 564 p. illus. 23 cm. 70/–

(B 68–17781)

"Distribution in the U. S. A. by Barnes and Noble."
Translation of Lumière et couleurs, published as v. 2 of the author's Optique physiologique.
Bibliography: p. 504–538.

1. Optics. Physiological. I. Title.

QP475.L473   1968   612'.84   68–68889

Shared Cataloging with   DNLM   BOS
Library of Congress   [2]

Card 60

French.

> If the prefix consists of a preposition or of a preposition followed by an article, enter under the part of the name following the preposition.

Aligny, Géraud d'.
    Sources et cascades. ₍Poëmes. St- Amand (Cher), Impr. Ch. -A. Bédu, 196₃₎
    61 p. illus. 23 cm.

Card 61

Balzac, Honoré de, 1799-1850.
    La cousine Bette ₍par ₎ H. de Balzac. ₍Introd., notes et relevé de variantes, par Maurice Allem, pseud. ₎ Paris, Garnier ₍1965, c1962 ₎
    xlii, 500 p. illus. 19 cm. (₍Classiques Garnier ₎)

Card 62

Gaulle, Charles de, 1890–
    War memoirs. New York, Viking Press, 1955–60.
    5v. illus.

Card 63

Hondt, Jacques d'.
    Hegel secret, recherches sur les sources cachées de la pensée de Hegel ... Paris, Presses universitaires de France, 1968.
    348 p. 18 cm. (Épiméthée; essais philosophiques) 24 F

                                    (F•••)

    Illustrated cover.
    Bibliographical footnotes.

Card 64

La Briere, Leon de, 1845–
    L'autre France; voyage au Canada. Paris, Dentu, 1886.
    149p.

Card 65

German.

> If the prefix consists of an article or of a con-
> traction of a preposition and an article, enter
> under the prefix. But, if the prefix consists of
> a preposition or a preposition followed by an
> article, enter under the part of the name follow-
> ing the prefix.

Bismarck, Klaus von, 1912-
    Probleme der Publizistik in Afrika; zwei
Vorträge, von Klaus von Bismarck und E. J. B.
Rose.   Assen, Van Gorcum, 1963.
    76 p. 18 cm. (Münsteraner Marginalien
zur Publizistik. Nr. 3)
    1. Information services—Africa. 2. Informa-
tion services—Germany.   I. Rose, E. J. B.
(Series)
NN   NUC66-77730

Card
66

Vom Endt, Rudolf.
    Knix und Knax; fröhliche abenteur
zwischen Nordpol und Südpol.   Essen,
Bildgut Verlag und Druckerei, 1934.
    109p. illus.

Card
67

Italian.

  Generally, all Italian names should be entered under the prefix.

D'Annunzio, Gabrielle, 1863-1938. **La fiaccola sotto il moggio.** **Roma, Mondadori, 1957.** **177p.**	Card 68
Della Rocca, Fernando. **America, spirito e azione.** **Milano, Sperling & Kupfer** /̲1957̲/ **228p. illus.**	Card 69
DeVito, Anthony Joseph. Le novelle di Salvatore di Giacomo. Napoli, Istituto meridionale de cultura ₁1962?₁ 48 p.	Card 70
Di Cesnola, Alessandro Palma, 1837- **Catalogo di manoscritti italiani** **esistenti nel Museo britannico de** **Londra. Torino, Roux, 1890.** **208p.**	Card 71
Lo Bianco, Giuseppe. **Bibliografia italiana dell'estimo.** /̲Palermo̲/ **1960.** **136p.**	Card 72

Portuguese.

Enter under the part of the name that follows the prefix.

Amaral, Diogo Freitas do.
  A utilização do domínio público pelos
particulares.   Lisboa [Coimbra] Editora, 1965.
293 p. , 2 l. 24 cm.

Card
73

Barros, Maria da Glória Lopes de, *comp.*
  Coletânea cívica [Pref. de Vittorio Bergo] Rio de
Janeiro, Freitas Bastos, 1967.
  182 p. illus. 23 cm. (Biblioteca pedagógica Freitas Bastos)

Card
74

Cunha, António Maria Santos da.
  A propósito da educação; dois discursos na
Assembleia nacional [do] António Maria Santos
da Cunha. Com um prefácio do Guilherme Braga
da Cruz.   Braga, Livraria Cruz, 1965.
59 p. 23 cm.

Card
75

Santos, Francisco Martins dos.
  Marques de Pombal. Apostilhas, feitas
sobre a sua vida. [Por] Prof. Martins dos
Santos.   [n. p. , Edição da Tip. "Noticiss da
Covilhã, 1960?]
  30 p. 21 cm.

Card
76

Martins, Myriam Gusmão de.
  Abordagem aos problemas bibliotecários; iniciação à
biblioteconomia numa área em desenvolvimento.   Recife,
Curso de Biblioteconomia, 1967.
  [23] p. illus. 32 cm. unpriced

(BBM 68-1467)

Card
77

1. Libraries Brazil. 2. Libraries and the socially handicapped—
Brazil.   i. Title. ii. Title: Iniciação à biblioteconomia numa área
em desenvolvimento.

Z769.A1M3

68–141834

Library of Congress   [18]

Spanish.

Enter under the part of the name that follows the prefix, except that if the prefix consists of an article only, enter under the article.

Cagigas, Isidoro de las
Tratados y convenios referentes
a Marruecos. Madrid, Instituto de
Estudios Africanos, 1952.
506p.

Card
78

Maza, Francisco de la, 1913–
La mitología clásica en el arte colonial de México. ₁1.
ed.₁ México, Universidad Nacional Autónoma de México,
1968.

251 p. illus., facsims. 24 cm. (Estudios y fuentes del arte en
México, 24)

Card
79

Monserrat, María de.
Con motivo de vivir; novela. Montevideo,
Editorial Alfa ₁1962₁
59 p. 20 cm. (Colección Letras de hoy, 9)

Card
80

Río Rodríguez, Luis Felipe del.
Geografía lírica de Coahuila. Saltillo, 1965.
1 v. (unpaged) illus. 25 cm. (Ediciones de
la Universidad de Coahuila)

Card
81

Roca, Julio César de la.
Tierranueva de Guatemala. Guatemala,
Tipografía Nacional, 1965.
80 p. illus. 21 cm. (Colección "Casa de la
Cultura de Occidente", no. 2)
"Bibliografía": p. 79-80.
1. Petén, Guatemala (Dept.)–Description and
travel. 2. Petén, Guatemala (Dept.)–History.
I. Title.
KU   NUC67-150

Card
82

46-G.   Titles of nobility, honor, address, etc. added
to names.

46-G-1.   Titles of nobility.

The title of nobility in the vernacular should be
added to the name of a nobleman who is not entered under
his title.

**Hood, Alexander Nelson, Duke of
Bronte, 1854–
Adria; a tale of Venice.**
New York, Dutton, 1904.
xiii, 447p. illus.

Card
83

Humboldt, Alexander, *Freiherr von,* 1769–1859.
The Humboldt Library; a catalogue of the library of
Alexander von Humboldt; with a bibliographical and bio-
graphical memoir by Henry Stevens. London, Henry
Stevens, American Agency, 1863. ₁Leipzig, Zentral-Anti-
quariat, 1967₁

9, 791 p. 22 cm. DM 176.–

(GDNB 68–A20–5)

Card
84

**Sadoine, Esther, Baroness
The reluctant lady; a novel by
the Baroness Albert Sadoine.**
London, Hutchinson, 1926.
280p.

Card
85

Zittel, Karl Alfred, Ritter von, 1839-1904.
Geschichte der Geologie und Paläontologie
bis Ende des 19. Jahrhunderts. München und
Leipzig, 1899, Druck und Verlag von R. Olden-
bourg. New York, Johnson Reprint Corp.
₁1965₁
xi, 868 p. (Geschichte der Wissenschaften
in Deutschland. Neuere Zeit. 23. Bd.)
"First reprinting. "
1. Geology—Hist. 2. Paleontology—Hist.
(Series)
ICU   NUC67-1418

Card
86

46-G-2. British titles of honor.

The four terms of honor which are to be used are:
"Sir", "Dame", "Lord" and "Lady". The term "Honorable",
usually abbreviated to "Hon." is no longer used and is
either replaced by one of the four terms mentioned above
or eliminated. The term of honor is added before the
forenames of the person. "Sir" is used for British bar-
onets and knights; "Dame" for the dames of the Order of
the British Empire and the Royal Victorian Order; "Lord"
for the younger sons of dukes and marquesses; and "Lady"
for the daughters of dukes, marquesses and earls. Add
after the forenames the titles of rank, "bart." in the
case of a baronet, and "Lady" for the wife of a baronet
or knight who is not entitled to the prefixed title of
"Lady" by virtue of her father's rank.

Sackville, Lady Margaret, 1881–
   Alicia and the twilight; a
fantasy by Margaret Sackville.
London, Gardner, Darton, 1928.
   vii, 96p.
	Card
	87

Mosley, Sir Oswald, bart., 1896–
   My life. London, Nelson, 1968.
   521p. illus.
	Card
	88

Gielgud, *Sir* **John,** 1904–
    Stage directions. New York, Random House ₁1964, °1963₁
    xiv, 146 p. illus., port. 22 cm.
	Card
	89

Chichester, *Sir* **Francis Charles,** 1901–
    'Gipsy Moth' circles the world, by Francis Chichester.
London, Hodder & Stoughton, 1967.
 	
    xvi, 269 p. 40 plates, illus. (incl. 8 col.), charts, facsims., plan,
ports. 23 cm. 35/–
    (SBN 340 00484 3)   (B 68–01645)
 	
    1. Voyages around the world—1951–   2. Gipsy Moth ɪv (Sail-
ing yacht)   ɪ. Title.
 	
    G420.C47A3 1967   910.4′1   68–88340
    Library of Congress   ₍3₎
	Card
	90

46-G-3. Terms of address of married women.

When a married woman is identified only by her husband's name include the term of address in the heading.

```
Henrey, Mrs. Robert, 1906-                          Card
     Paloma.  New York, Dutton,                      91
1955.
     256p.
```

```
Roadknight, Mrs., comp.
     Old-fashioned rhymes & poems.
Selected by Mrs. Roadknight.  London,
New York, Longmans, Green, 1906.
     x, 96p.                                         Card
                                                      92
```

47. Entry under title of nobility.

Enter a nobleman under the proper name in his title of nobility if he uses his title rather than his surname in his works, or if he is generally so listed in those reference sources that do not list noblemen either all under title or all under surname.

```
Berkeley, Mary Emlen Lloyd, Countess of Berkeley.
     Winking at the brim [by] Molly Berkeley.  With a fore-
word by L. P. Hartley.  Illustrated with photos.  Boston,
Houghton Mifflin, 1967.
     xx, 172 p.  illus., ports.  22 cm.                     Card
     London ed. ( H. Hamilton) has title: Beaded bubbles.    93


     I. Title.
CT788.B452A3  1967      828'.9'1403        67-16813


     Library of Congress         [5]
```

Radcliffe, Cyril John Radcliffe, *1st Viscount*, 1899–
 Not in feather beds: some collected papers ₁by₁ the Viscount Radcliffe. London, H. Hamilton, 1968.

 xviii, 277 p. col. port. 23 cm. 42/-

 SBN 241-01590-1   (B 68-20066)

                                                                            Card
                                                                            94

 ɪ. Title.

 AC8.R14   082   **77–35**⁹
                                            FEB 1 4 '69 **AD**

 Library of Congress   69 ₁18₁

Wicklow. William Cecil James Philip John Paul
 Howard. 8th Earl of, 1902–
    Life after death: an anthology, edited and
 compiled by the Earl of Wicklow.   London,
 Burns, Oates & Washbourne; Dublin,   Clonmore
 & Reynolds. 1959.
    117 p.
    1. Future life–Catholic authors.   I. Title.
 CLamB   NUC66-61788

                                                                            Card
                                                                            95

Windlesham, David James George Hennessy, *Baron*, 1932–
   Communication and political power ₁by₁ Lord Windlesham. London, Cape, 1966.

   288 p. 8 tables. 22½ cm. 45/-
                                                      (B 66-14271)
   Bibliographical footnotes.
                                                                            Card
                                                                            96

   1. Communication. 2. Electioneering—Gt. Brit. 3. Public relations and politics.   ɪ. Title.

 HM258.W5   301.1523   66–73811

 Library of Congress   ₁5₁

49. Entry under given name or byname.

49-A. General rules.

A person whose name does not include a surname and who is not primarily identified by a title of nobility should be entered under the part of the name by which he is primarily identified in reference sources, normally the first part of the names that he uses.

Dante Alighieri, 1265-1321.
  The Divine Comedy: the Inferno, Purgatorio, and Paradiso. A new translation into English blank verse, by Lawrence Grant White, with illus. by Gustave Doré. New York, Pantheon Books, 1965.
    xiv, 187 p. plates. 27 cm.

Card 97

Moses ben Maimon, 1135-1204.
  The Book of Holiness, translated from the Hebrew by Louis I. Rabinowitz and Philip Grossman. New Haven, Yale University Press, 1965.
    429 p. (Yale Judaica series, 16)

Card 98

Thomas à Kempis, 1380-1471.
  In praise of the Blessed Virgin. Translated by Robert E. Patterson. Milwaukee, Bruce Pub. Co. /1956/
    52p.

Card 99

Tōshūsai Sharaku, fl. 1794.
  Sharaku ₁by Elise Grilli. English ed. ₁
New York, Crown Publishers ₁c1962₁
    32 p. 30 plates (part col.) (Art of the East library)
    Bibliography: p. 32.
    1. Color prints, Japanese.   I. Grilli, Elise.
  CLU   NUC67-1746

Card 100

49-B. Royalty.

Add the title in English (unless there is no satis-
factory English equivalent) and the name of the state or
people governed after the name of a monarch.

Charles I, *King of Great Britain,* 1600–1649.
  The letters, speeches, and proclamations.   Edited by Sir
Charles Petrie. New York, Funk & Wagnalls ₁1968₁

  xv, 319 p. geneal. table, port. 22 cm. 6.95

  Bibliography: p. 309.

Card
101

Elizabeth I, Queen of England, 1533-1603.
  /Correspondence7
  The letters of Queen Elizabeth I.
Edited by G. B. Harris. New York,
Funk & Wagnalls /c19687
  xvi, 323p. illus.

Card
102

Henry VIII, King of England, 1491-1547.
  /Correspondence7
  The letters of King Henry VIII: a
selection, with a few other documents.
Edited by M. St. Clare Byrne. New
York, Funk & Wagnalls /c19687
  454p. illus.

Card
103

Manuel II, Palaeologus, Emperor of the East,
  1350-1425.
    Dialoge mit einem "Perser" ₁hrsg. von₁
Erich Trapp. Wien, In Kommission bei
H. Böhlaus, Nachf., 1966.
    95, 318 p. facsims. (Wiener byzantinistische
Studien, Bd. 2)
    Text in Greek.
    Includes bibliography.
    I. Trapp, Erich, ed. II. Title.   (Series)
  ICU NNC   NUC66-84446

Card
104

49-C. Saints

Add the word "Saint" after the name of a Christain
saint unless the person was an emperor, king or pope, in
which case that is the only identifying phrase used after
his name. Previously, monarchs and popes would have both
designations after their names if they were also saints,
but the AA rules have eliminated placing both designations
after the name.

John of the Cross, Saint, 1542-1591.
  Cántico espiritual y poesía de
San Juan de la Cruz, según el códice
de Sanlúcar de Barrameda. Burgos,
Tipografía "El Monte Carmelo", 1928.
  2v.

Card
105

Teresa, Saint, 1515-1582.
  **Interior castle. Translated and
edited by E. Allison Peers, from the
critical edition of P. Silverio de
Santa Teresa. Garden City, N.Y.,
Doubleday** ⁄1961⁄
  235p.

Card
106

Thomas Aquinas, *Saint*, 1225?-1274.
  Tractatus de substantiis separatis. A newly-established
Latin text based on 12 mediaeval mss., with introd. and
notes by Francis J. Lescoe. West Hartford, Conn., Saint
Joseph College ₁1962₁

  x, 207 p. facsims. 24 cm.

  Bibliography : p. 181-189.

  1. Substance (Philosophy) 2. Angels—Early works to 1800.
ɪ. Lescoe, Francis J., ed. ɪɪ. Title.

B765.T53T7 1962   62-12144

Library of Congress   ₁5₁

Card
107

49-D. Popes.

    Add the appropriate designation, in English, after
the pontifical name assumed by a pope or antipope. The
name of the pope should be in an English form, when there
is one. For those who have the same name add after the
name the Roman numeral by which each is identified.

John XXIII, Pope, 1881-1963.
    Journal of a soul. Translated
by Dorothy White. New York,
McGraw-Hill /1965/
    lvii, 453p. illus.

Card
108

Paul VI, Pope, 1897-
    Man's religious sense; a pastoral
letter written as Cardinal Archbishop
of Milan by Giovanni Battista Montini,
now His Holiness Pope Paul VI. London,
Darton, Longman & Todd, 1965.
    64p.

Card
109

49-E. Bishops, cardinals, etc.

After the name of a bishop, archbishop, cardinal,
metropolitan or other such high ecclesiastical official
who is entered under the given name or byname add the
appropriate title, in English, if possible. If he has
had more than one such title, use only the one of the
highest rank.

The idea of highest rank or uniqueness of a title
is intimated in the choice of a monarchial or papal designation instead of that of saint. The AA rules have tried
to avoid the use of multiple designations after a person's
name which make simpler headings and eliminate certain
filing rules.

Colonna, Egidio, *Abp., d.* 1316.
    B. Ægidii Columnæ Romani Quodlibeta. Frankfurt/
Main, Minerva, 1966.

    ₍16₎, 468 p. port. 30 cm.

    "Unveränderter Nachdruck."
    Original t. p. reads: B. Ægidii Colvmnæ Romani ... Quodlibeta.
Revisa, correcta, et varie illvstrata stvdio Petri Damasi de Coninck.
Lovanii, Typis H. Nempæi, 1646.
    "Scripta Ægidii Columnij": prelim. p. ₍12₎–₍13₎

Card
110

Patrick, Simon, Bp. of Ely, 1626-1707.
    The auto-biography of Symon Patrick,
bishop of Ely, now first printed from the
original manuscript.   Oxford, Parker,
1839.   ₍Cleveland, Ohio, Bell & Howell,
Micro Photo Div., 1965?₎
    291 p. 23 cm.

Card
111

Mathew, David, *Abp.,* 1902–
    Lord Acton and his times. London, Eyre & Spottiswoode,
1968.

    397 p. plate, map, port. 23 cm. 70/-
                                   (B 68-24945)

    Bibliography: p. 375-377.

Card
112

    1. Acton, John Emerich Edward Dalberg Acton, Baron, 1834-1902.
I. Title.

D15.A25M32   907'.2'024 (B)   73-365417

    Library of Congress   69 ₍2₎

49-F. Other persons of religious vocation.

For any other person of religious vocation who is entered under given name or byname, add either the vernacular term of honor or address or the vernacular title to the name, whether or not it is the religious name.

Antoninus, *Brother,* 1912–
　　The residual years; poems 1934–1948. The pre-Catholic poetry of Brother Antoninus ₍by₎ William Everson. With an introd. by Kenneth Rexroth. ₍New York, New Directions, 1968₎

　　　xvii, 238 p.　21 cm.　(A New Directions book)　$6.50

Card 113

Jeanne Marie, Sister.
　　Maryknoll's first lady.　New York, Dodd, Mead, 1964.
　　327 p.　illus.

Card 114

Mary Louise, *Sister,* D. C.
　　The operating room technician.　2d ed.　Saint Louis, Mosby, 1968.

　　　xviii, 282 p.　illus.　26 cm.

　　　Includes bibliographical references.

Card 115

Mary Paula of the Blessed Trinity, Sister.
　　Statistics notebook.　The sociology of religion.　₍New York₎ 1961.
　　1 v. (unpaged)　tables.　28 cm.

Card 116

Regis, *Sister,* 1908–　　*ed.*
　　The Catholic bookman's guide; a critical evaluation of Catholic literature.　Contributors: Vernon J. Bourke ₍and others. 1st ed.₎ New York, Hawthorn Books ₍1962₎

　　　638 p.　24 cm.

Card 117

　　　1. Catholic literature—Bibl.　2. Catholic literature—Hist. & crit.　ɪ. Title.

　　Z7837.R37　　　　　　016.80889　　　　　　62–12956

　　Library of Congress　　　　₍5₎

50. Entry of Roman names.

For a Roman of classical times whose name has no
established form in English the entry should be made under
the part of his name most commonly used as entry element
in reference sources. In case of doubt, entry should be
made under the first of his names.

Catullus, C. Valerius.
   Poems. Translated and with an
introduction by Horace Gregory.
New York, Grove Press /c1956/
   xxiv, 184p.

Card
118

Persius Flaccus, Aulus.
   Satires. Translated by W. S.
Merwin. Introduction & notes by
William S. Anderson. Bloomington,
Indiana University Press, 1961.
   119p.

Card
119

Tacitus, Cornelius.
   The annals of imperial Rome. A new
translation with an introduction by
Michael Grant. /Baltimore/ Penguin
Books /1956/

   447p. illus.

Card
120

51. <u>Entry under phrase</u>.

      A person who is always identified in his works or
in reference sources by an appellation or pseudonym consisting of a word, phrase, or expression that is obviously
not intended to be taken as a real name, should be entered
under this appellation or pseudonym in direct order. But,
if it has the structure of a real name consisting of a
forename, or forenames and a surname then treat it like a
real name and invert it. Make a reference from this type
of appellation in its direct order.

Aunt Ruth.
    Adventures of an old maid.
New York, J. S. Ogilvie /c1886/
    183p. illus.

Card
121

Old Sarge.
    How to get along in the army,
by "Old Sarge". New York, Appleton-
Century, 1942.
    x, 168p. illus.

Card
122

Pound Sterling.
    Camp fires of the Twenty-third;
sketches of the camp life, marches,
and battles of the Twenty-third
regiment, N.Y.V. New York, Davies &
Kent, printers, 1863.
    viii, 196p.

Card
123

Uncle Spike.
    Negro history tour of Manhattan,
by Uncle Spike, the Negro history
detective. New York, Negro History
Associates, 1967.
    i, 65 ℓ.

Card
124

52. _Dates._

The years of a person's birth and death are not considered as an essential part of the heading for an individual and ·should be added only if they are readily ascertainable at the time the heading is established, or if it is necessary to distinguish between two individuals with identical names.

The British text of the AA rules does not recommend that dates always be used even if they are readily ascertainable, but rather only in those cases where it is necessary to distinguish between different persons of the same name.

Brushfield, Thomas Nadauld, 1828–1910.
    A bibliography of Sir Walter Ralegh, knt. New York, B. Franklin ₍1968₎

181 p. illus., facsims., ports. 24 cm. (Burt Franklin bibliography and reference series, #175)

Reprint of the 2d ed., 1908.

Card 125

Hope, Bob, 1903–
    I never left home, by Bob Hope, illustrated by Carl Rose. New York, Simon and Schuster ₍1944₎

viii p., 1 l., 207, ₍2₎ p. illus. 21½ᶜᵐ.

Card 126

Ashton, John, _b._ 1834, _ed._
    Chap-books of the eighteenth century. New York, B. Blom ₍1966₎

xvi, 486 p. facsims. 23 cm.

Card 127

McCalmon, George, _d._ 1965.
    Creating historical drama; a guide for the community and the interested individual, by George McCalmon and Christian Moe. Foreword by Louis C. Jones. Carbondale, Southern Illinois University Press ₍1965₎

xvi, 393 p. illus. 23 cm.

Bibliography: p. 369–380.

1. Historical drama—Hist. & crit.   2. Theater—Production and direction.   I. Moe, Christian Hollis, 1929–
II. Title.

PN1872.M3   792.02   65–12501

Library of Congress   ₍3₎

Card 128

Walpole, Arthur Sumner, 1850 *or* 1–1920, *ed.*
Early Latin hymns with introduction and notes by the late
A. S. Walpole, M. A. Cambridge ₁Eng.₁ The University press,
1922.

xxviii, 445. ₁1₁ p. 19½ᶜᵐ. (*Half-title:* Cambridge patristic texts)

Card
129

Nelson, Thomas, Apr. 24, 1872–
Practical textile designing, by Thomas Nelson ... **Charlotte,**
N. C., Clark publishing company, ᶜ1945.

168. ₁2₁ p. 20ᶜᵐ.

Card
130

Lydgate, John, 1370?-1451?
The dyetary; or, The medecine of the
stomach; as printed by William Caxton in
1489. ₁Oxford, Bodleian Library, 1963₁
facsim. (₁6₁ p.), ₁2₁ p.

Card
131

Stewart, Margaret, *fl.* 1938–
Frank Cousins: a study. London, Hutchinson, 1968.

xiv, 210 p. 7 plates, illus., ports. 22 cm. 35/-

(SBN 09 087030 1)   (B 68–08604)

Bibliography: p. ₁203₁–204.

Card
132

Soria, Francesco Antonio, *ca.* 1730–1799.
Memorie storico-critiche degli storici napolitani. Bologna,
Forni, 1967.

x, 684 p. 25 cm. unpriced   It 67–10137

Facsim. of the 1781–1782 Naples ed.

Card
133

Fugger, Wolfgang, *16th cent.*
Ein nützlich und wolgegründt Formular manncherley
schöner Schriefften. Vollständige Faksimileausg. des
Schreibmeisterbuchs von 1553, mit einem Nachwort von
Friedrich Pfäfflin. München-Pullach, Verlag Dokumenta-
tion ₁ᶜ1967₁

224 p. illus. 15 x 22 cm.

1. Penmanship.   2. Alphabets.   3. Lettering.   I. Title.

Z43.A3F8   1967   68–131196

Library of Congress   ₁2₁

Card
134

53. Distinguishing terms.

Terms are added to a person's name only when a word or phrase is necessary to distinguish between persons of identical names for whom no dates are available. This precludes the addition of a phrase just to indicate that a person held a high office or rank.

E.g. Nixon, Richard Milhous, 1913-

not

Nixon, Richard Milhous, Pres. U.S., 1913-

However, titles of nobility and honor are still used as illustrated in the examples given under rules 46, 47 and 49.

Henderson, John, capt. 78th Highlanders.
    Observations on the colonies of New
South Wales and Van Diemen's Land.
Calcutta, Baptist Mission Press, 1832.
[Adelaide, Libraries Board of South
Australia, 1965]
    xxv, 180 p. illus. 22 cm.

Card
135

Hunt, Peter, *of Provincetown, Mass.*
    Peter Hunt's workbook, with text and pictures. Chicago,
New York, Ziff-Davis publishing company [1945]

2 p. l., vii-x, 100 p. illus. (part col., incl. ports.) 29^{cm}.

Card
136

Roger, Pierre, writer on chemistry.
    Chimie organique.   Paris, J. B. Baillière
[1966]
    392 p. illus., port. 24 cm. (Collection de
Sciences physiques)

Card
137

Siqueira, Antonio de, *civil engineer.*
    Engenharia sanitaria; higiene da água, higiene do solo,
higiene do ar, higiene individual. 2. ed. Rio de Janeiro,
Editôra Globo [1959]

2 v. illus. 24 cm.

1. Sanitary engineering.

TD145.S5 1959

61-29151 ‡

Library of Congress   [1]

Card
138

Queen, Ellery
 The glass village, a novel.
Boston, Little, Brown, 1954.
 281p.

Queen, Ellery, Jr.
 The blue herring mystery.
Boston, Little, Brown, 1954.
 214p.

Langlois, Pierre, *of Paris.*
 Guide bibliographique des études littéraires [par] Pierre
Langlois ... André Mareuil ... 3ᵉ édition revue ... **Paris,**
Hachette, 1965.

 296, xxxv p. 20 cm. 15.50 F.

              (F 67–3500)

Lucas, Heinz, writer on masks.
 Japanische Kultmasken; der Tanz der Krani-
che. Kassel, E. Röth [1965]
 222 p. illus. (part col.) map. 24 cm.

Richter, Walter, horticulturist.
 The orchid world. Translated and revised by
Edmund Launert, edited by P. Francis Hunt.
[London] Studio Vista [1965]
 291 p. illus.

Poll, Max, *doctor of natural sciences.*
 Une famille dulcicole nouvelle de poissons africains: les
Congothrissidae, par M. Poll. Brussel, Koninklijke Aca-
demie voor Overzeese Wetenschappen, 1964.
  40 p. illus., plates. 25 cm. (Académie royale des sciences
d'outre-mer. Classe des sciences naturelles et médicales. [Mémoires
in 8.] n. s. 15–2)
  Summary in French and Flemish.
  Bibliography: p. [36]–37.

  1. Congothrissidae. 2. Fishes, Fresh-water—Africa, Central. I.
Title. (Series: Académie royale des sciences d'outre-mer. Classe
des sciences naturelles et médicales. Mémoires. Verhandelingen.
In-8°. Nouv. sér., t. 15, fasc. 2)

Q111.B78 n. S., t. 15, fasc. 2   66–58759

CHAPTER II

GENERAL RULES FOR DETERMINING MAIN AND ADDED ENTRIES
Rules 1-19 and 33

In the introductory notes to this chapter in the AA rules it is suggested that the designations of function, such as "joint author" and "joint compiler" are not necessary. Since most libraries follow the logical practice of interfiling headings for the same person by disregarding the various designations such as "comp.", "ed.", "illus." and "tr.", there is really no practical value in adding the terms "jt. author", "jt. compiler", or "jt. editor". Never more than one term is used following a heading, e.g. the heading for an anthology compiled and illustrated by the same person would only show the person as a compiler. Previously terms were combined to form such designations as "comp. and illus.", but this proved unsatisfactory.

In the British text the designations of function, "comp.", "ed.", "illus." and "tr." are mentioned with the phrase that they "may be added", while the North American text states that "an abbreviated designation is added". Thus the British consider even these very basic designations as definitely non-essential.

The nineteen general rules of the first chapter in the AA rules deal with the manner of determining who or what is responsible for the contents of a publication and not the form in which the entry is to be written. The correct form of personal names is covered in Chapter II, and of corporate names in Chapter III of the <u>Anglo-American Cataloging Rules</u>.

1. <u>Works of single authorship</u>.

The basic principle used in determining the main entry is to establish which person or corporate body is responsible for the contents of the publication. This rule illustrates a very basic cataloging principle.

It should be noted at this point that usually the exact form of the entry is not given in the examples used anywhere in the AA rules, but rather only an indication as to which person or entity is the one to be treated as main entry, e.g. "Main entry under Hemingway", and "Main entry under the institute". In many cases it would have been clearer to the cataloger if the examples would have been cited in the following manner:

"Main entry: Hemingway, Ernest, 1899-1961."
"Main entry: Detroit Institute of Arts."

2. <u>Works of unknown or uncertain authorship, or by un-named groups.</u>

2-A. Any work which has no known author or one that is not attributed to anyone should be entered under its title. Works of uncertain authorship which have editions with varying authors named on the title pages should also be entered under the title and added entries made for no more than three individuals to whom authorship has been attributed. This principle is also applied to those publications whose authorship is attributed to a group that has no name. In more and more cases entry is now being made under title, and this is a very practical approach as the title is probably the one piece of information which varies the least and at the same time the one most often available to the cataloger and most often known to the user of the library. This is a definite improvement over devising an entry or arbitrarily choosing one name over another one which would cause variations in the entry for the same publication in libraries.

Whenever a publication has its main entry under the title the card form used is that of "hanging indention".

```
Old Fort Duquesne, a tale of the
    early toils, struggles and
    adventures of the first settlers
    at the forks of the Ohio, 1754.
    Pittsburgh, Cook's Literary Depot,      Card
    1844.                                    145
    79p.
```

A **State** of the whole people; a collection of essays by Soviet commentators. London ₍Soviet Booklets₎ 1962.

23 p. 22 cm. (Soviet booklet no. 86)

Card
146

Federal aid for all the schools. ₍New York, America Press, 1962₎

64 p. illus. 20 cm.

Card
147

1. Federal aid to education. 2. Church and education in the U. S.
3. Catholic Church in the U. S.—Education.

LC111.F4   379.12   62–3882 ‡

Library of Congress   ₍2₎

2-C. Often the only clue to authorship is the appearance
on the title page of initials, some other alphabetical
device, a characterizing word or phrase preceded by an
indefinite article, or a phrase in which another work that
the author wrote is mentioned, in which cases the work is
to be entered under the title. Added entries are made for
these various devices, but if the only clue to the authorship is a non-alphabetical typographical device no added
entry is made. According to the ALA rules added entries
were always made for any type of typographical device,
even when the added entry was for a translator or an illustrator. For some excellent examples of this type of added
entry see pages 1-8 of Volume One of the National union
catalog, pre-1956 imprints, (London, Mansell, 1968).

Right & wrong in the Ruhr Valley;
a study of the legal aspect of
the Franco-Belgian occupation
of the Ruhr, by **** . London,
British Periodicals Ltd., 1923.
42p.

Card
148

Summer days in Auvergne, by H. de K.
London, Bentley, 1875.
170p. illus.

Card
149

A Sweetheart for somebody, a
novel. By the author of
"Margaret's engagement".
New York, Carleton, 1878.
192p.

Card
150

Tales of the revolution, by a young
gentleman of Nashville. Nashville,
Hunt, Tardiff, 1833.
179p.

Card
151

The Story of Oscar Wilde's life and
experience in Reading Gaol, by
his warder. With a tribute by
Rose Freeman-Ishill. Berkeley
Heights, N.J., Oriole Pr., 1963.
21p.

Card
152

3. Works of shared authorship.

This rule applies to: (1) Works produced by the joint collaboration of two or more authors. (2) Works for which different authors have prepared separate contributions, as long as the authors are not acting as members of a corporate body in which case rule 17 would be applied. Those which are included here are composite works, symposia, series of addresses, lectures, etc. which were written specifically for a particular occasion or for the publication in hand. This can include certain Festschrifts, which are honorary or memorial collections containing contributions written by various persons to commemorate or celebrate a particular occasion or anniversary of a person, an institution or a society. (3) Works consisting of correspondence, debates, etc. between different persons.

All of the provisions of this rule for works of shared authorship are applied equally to all cases of shared responsibility among compilers, editors, translators, adapters, illustrators, etc. when the applicable rule indicates that the main entry is to be made under such a person.

3-A. Principal author indicated.

A work produced by shared authorship should be entered under the person or corporate body to whom principal responsibility is attributed. The principal author can be indicated or signified by wording, typography, or position on the title page.

```
Saunders, Hugh
    Observations and studies in child
development, by Hugh Saunders with
the assistance of Richard Hunter,
Walter McNamee, Lawrence Smith and      Card
Paul Spector.  London, Maclaren, 1959.   153
    xii, 342p.
```

3-B.   Principal author not indicated.

3-B-1.   When there is no indication that one person is more responsible than the others, and there are no more than three authors, the main entry is under the one named first on the title page.

Hunt, Kenneth Edward.
　　The state of British agriculture, 1959–60, by K. E. Hunt and K. R. Clark.   Oxford, University of Oxford, Agricultural Economics Research Institute, 1960.

　　　viii, 151 p.   diagrs., tables.   22 cm.
　　　Bibliographical footnotes.

Card 154

Hunt, Robert Lee.
　　Effects of angling regulations on a wild brook trout fishery, by Robert L. Hunt, Oscar M. Brynildson, and James T. McFadden.   Madison, Wisconsin Conservation Dept., 1962.

　　　58 p.   illus.   23 cm.   (Wisconsin. Conservation Dept. Technical bulletin no. 26)

Card 155

Thomason, Oliver Bruce, *ed.*
　　Casework performance in vocational rehabilitation; compiled from proceedings of guidance, training, and placement workshops.   Edited by Bruce Thomason and Albert M. Barrett.   ₁Washington, U. S. Dept. of Health, Education, and Welfare, Office of Vocational Rehabilitation, 1959 ₁i. e. 1960₁
　　　vii, 59 p.   24 cm.   (U. S.   Office of Vocational Rehabilitation. GTP bulletin no. 1.   Rehabilitation service series, no. 505)
　　　Includes bibliographies.

Card 156

Stacey, Maurice, 1907–
　　Carbohydrates of living tissues ₁by₁ M. Stacey ₁and₁ S. A. Barker.   London, New York, Van Nostrand ₁1962₁

　　　215 p.   illus.   24 cm.

Card 157

　　　1. Mucopoly saccharides.　　ɪ. Barker, Sidney Alan
　　ɪɪ. Title.

QP701.S8   1962　　　　　　612.015　　　　　　61–14612 ‡

　　Library of Congress　　　　　₁10₁

3-B-2. When no one is indicated as principal author and there are four or more authors, the work is entered under its title. Make an added entry under the first named author. This rule does not apply to those works produced under the direction of an editor who is named on the title page, in which case apply the provisions of rule 4.

Outside readings in American govern-
     ment /by/ H. Malcolm MacDonald,
     Wilfred D. Webb, Edward G. Lewis
     /and/ William L. Strauss. New
     York, Crowell /c1949/
     x, 854p.

Card
158

Developing a curriculum for modern
     living /by/ Florence B. Strate-
     meyer, Hamden L. Forkner, Margaret
     G. McKim and cooperating members
     of the Childhood-Youth Education
     Committee, Thompsie Baxter, Mary
     Ella Chayer / and others / New
     York, Teachers College, Columbia
     University /c1947/
     xiii, 558p.

Card
159

Economic development issues: Latin America ₍by₎ Roberto
    Alemann ₍and others. New York₎ Committee for Eco-
    nomic Development, 1967.
        xii, 340 p. illus. 23 cm. (Committee for Economic Development.
    Supplementary paper no. 21)
        "The outgrowth of the work of CED's Subcommittee on Develop-
    ment Policy."
        Bibliographical footnotes.
        CONTENTS.—Foreword, by R. Blough.—Economic development of
    Argentina, by R. Alemann.—Key factors in Chilean economic devel-
    opment, by S. Undurraga Saavedra.—Economic development of Co-
    lombia, by H. Echavarría. — Economic development of Mexico: fi-
    nancing the infrastructure, by G. Romero Kolbeck.—Economic devel-
    opment of Peru, by R. A. Ferrero. — Brazilian inflation: postwar
    experience and outcome of the 1964 reforms, by M. H. Simonsen.
        1. Latin America—   Economic policy—Addresses, essays,
    lectures.   I. Alemann,   Roberto T. II. Committee for Eco-
    nomic Development.   Subcommittee on Development Policy.
    HC125.E37   330.98   67-29353
    Library of Congress   ₍110-2₎

Card
160

4. Works produced under editorial direction.

This rule does not apply to serials, or to works which involve questions of corporate authorship, other than the responsibility of the publisher.

4-A. To determine that a work produced under editorial direction should be entered under the editor, examine the work to make sure that: (1) the editor is anemed on the title page, (2) the publisher is NOT named in the title, and (3) the editor appears to be primarily responsible for the existence of the work.

The presence of an editor's name on the title page does not necessarily indicate that he is primarily responsible for the existence of the work. Relevant information appearing anywhere in the work must be taken into account in the application of this rule. In the absence either of a positive or a negative statement in the work concerning editorial responsibility, the cataloger must make a judgment. Positive answers to one or both of the following questions strongly indicate responsibility which would warrant putting the main entry under the editor: (1) Does the person named as editor appear to have conceived the work, planned it, and selected the writers of the individual chapters, articles, etc.? , (2) In the case of composite works, have the individual parts been so developed and combined that the complete work forms a systematic treatment of the subject? If the editor's responsibility appears to be largely confined to the technical editing of the manuscript for publication, his responsibility is not sufficient to warrant main entry. In case of doubt the entry should be under the title.

If the above three qualifications fit the work in hand, then the main entry is under the editor. But, if any one of the three qualifications is not met, then the publication is entered under it title. Typical of the publications which are often produced under editorial direction are dictionaries, encyclopedias, festschrifts, etc.

Landau, Thomas, *ed.*
    Encyclopaedia of librarianship. 3d rev. ed. New York, Hafner Pub. Co., 1966 [ᶜ1958]

      x, 484 p. 26 cm.

Card 161

Stevenson, George A
    Graphic arts encyclopedia [by] George A. Stevenson. New York, McGraw-Hill [1968]

      xv, 492 p. illus. 24 cm.

      Bibliography : p. 421–422.

Card 162

    1. Printing—Dictionaries. 2. Graphic arts—Dictionaries.
    I. Title.

Z118.S82   655'.003   67–24445

Library of Congress   [15-2]

Searchlights on delinquency; new psychoanalytic studies
dedicated to Professor August Aichhorn on the occasion of
his seventieth birthday, July 27, 1948. Managing editor:
K. R. Eissler; chairman of the editorial board: Paul Federn.
New York, International Universities Press [1949]

xiii, 456 p. port. 24 cm.

Includes "References." "Bibliography of August Aichhorn's writings" : p. 455–456.

Card
163

Librarianship in Canada, 1946–1967; essays in honour of
Elizabeth Homer Morton; edited by Bruce Peel. Victoria,
B. C., printed for the Canadian Library Association by the
Morriss Printing Co., 1968.

205 p. 24 cm. unpriced

(C***)

Added t. p. in French: Le bibliothécariat au Canada de 1946 à
1967.
English or French.
Includes bibliographies.

1. Libraries—Canada—Addresses, essays, lectures.   I. Morton,
Elizabeth Homer. II. Peel, Bruce Braden, 1916–   ed. III. Title:
Le bibliothécariat au Canada de 1946 à 1967.

Card
164

A **List** of his writings presented to H. S. Bennett on his
eightieth birthday, 15 January 1969. London, Cambridge
U. P., 1969.

15 p. 2 ports. 21 cm. 5/- ($1.00)   B 69–04772

Card
165

The **Random House** vest pocket dictionary of famous people.
Edited by Constance Urdang. New York, Random House
[1962]

320 p. 15 cm.

1. Biography—Dictionaries.   I. Urdang, Constance, ed.

CT103.R23   920.02   62–9868

Library of Congress   [5]

Card
166

5. <u>Collections</u>.

For the purposes of this rule the following definitions should be used, (1) a collection is a publication which contains independently written works of two or more authors, and (2) a collective title is an inclusive title that covers the entire contents of a publication containing works of two or more authors.

All collections or anthologies of independent and previously existing works not written specifically for the same occasion, or for the work in hand can be divided into the following three groups and treated as indicated. Those works which are written for a single occasion or with the intention of being published together are to be entered according to the provisions of either rule 3 or rule 4.

5-A-1. Collections with a collective title and a compiler or editor are to be entered under the compiler or editor.

Brewton, Sara Westbrook, *comp.*
    Bridled with rainbows; poems about many things of earth and sky, selected by Sara and John E. Brewton. Decorations by Vera Bock. New York, Macmillan Co., 1949.
    xix, 191 p. illus. 24 cm.

Card 167

Baker, Augusta, *comp.*
    The talking tree; fairy tales from 15 lands. Illustrated by Johannes Troyer. ₁1st ed.₁ Philadelphia, Lippincott ₁1955₁
    255 p. illus. 23 cm.

Card 168

Landis, Paul, ed.
    Six plays by Corneille and Racine. Edited and with an introduction by Professor Paul Landis. New York, Modern Library /c1931/
        xii, 370p.

Card 169

If the compiler also translated the collection, only the designation "comp." is used in the heading.

Romskaug, Brenda, comp.
  Norwegian fairy tales. Selected
and translated by Brenda and Reidar
Romskaug. Illustrated by Ivar
Petterson. /Chester Springs, Pa./
Dufour Editions /1963, c1961/
  128p. illus.

Card
170

5-A-2. Collections with a collective title, but with no compiler or editor are to be entered under the title.

---

3 short novels, by Douglas Fairbairn, Blair Fuller, and
  George Mandel. New York, Random House [1961]

  246 p. 21 cm.

  CONTENTS.—The voice of Charlie Pont, by D. Fairbairn.—A butter-
  fly net and a kingdom, by B. Fuller.—Into the woods of the world, by
  G. Mandel.

Card
171

---

3 x 3: Stairway to the sea, by Thomas Firth Jones. This
  night in Sodom, by Charles Jules Reiter. Custom, by John
  Schultz. New York, Grove Press [1962]

  186 p. 22 cm.

  1. American fiction—20th cent.   I. Jones, Thomas Firth, 1934–
  Stairway to the sea.

  PZ1.T397   61–11771 ‡

  Library of Congress   [3]

Card
172

5-B. Collections without a collective title, irrespective
of the fact that there may or may not be a compiler or
editor are to be entered under the first named author on
the collective title page. If there is no collective title
page the main entry is made under the author of the first
work in the publication.

Thomas, John Hunter.
  The Gautier Herbarium [by] John H. Thomas. The history of botanical collecting in the Santa Cruz Mountains of
central California [by] John H. Thomas. A note on the
reported chromosome numbers for the genus *Larrea* [by]
Duncan M. Porter. Stanford, Calif., Natural History Museum of Stanford University, 1961.
    144-[169] p. 24 cm. (Contributions from the Dudley Herbarium,
v. 5, no. 6)
    Includes bibliographies.
    1. Botany — California — Santa Cruz Mountains. 2. Larrea. 3.
Chromosome numbers.   (Series: Stanford University. Dudley,
Herbarium. Contributions, v. 5, no. 6)

[QK1.S86 vol. 5,   no. 6]   A 62–3016

Stanford University.   **Libraries**
for Library of Congress   [3]

Card
173

Without editor or compiler and no collective title.

Eliot, George, 1819-1880
  Silas Marner, by George Eliot. The pearl,
by John Steinbeck. Edited by Jay E. Greene.
New York, Noble and Noble [1953]
  451p. illus. 20cm.

Card
174

With editor but no collective title.

6. <u>Serials</u>.

This one rule covers all classes of serials regardless of their type or source, which is quite unlike the ALA rules which depended on either the source of the serial, or its type for determining the main entry. This rule divides all serial publications into three groups: (1) those which are not issued by a corporate body and are not of personal authorship; and which are generally the product of a publishing firm and are published more as a business enterprise rather than to express the ideas and/or functions of a corporate body, (2) those issued by a corporate body, and (3) serials by a personal author. The main entry is then determined by the following guidelines for each of the three groups.

6-A.   Serials not issued by a corporate body and not of personal authorship.

Any serial that falls into this group is entered under its title, which in most cases is the only possible choice.

Dance magazine. v.1- June, 1927- /New York, R. Orthwine, etc./ v. illus. monthly.	Card 175
Holiday. v.1- June, 1945- Philadelphia, Curtis Pub. Co. v. illus. monthly.	Card 176
Life. v.1- Nov. 23, 1936- Chicago, Time, Inc. v. illus. weekly.	Card 177

6-B. Serials issued by a corporate body.

6-B-1. Into this category fall all serials issued by or
under the authority of a corporate body, including governments and governmental agencies. Serials issued by a
corporate body may be entered either under the title or
the name of the corporate body. The main entry is under
title unless (a) the title contains the full name or an
abbreviation (including the initials) of the full name
of the issuing body or the body of which the issuing body
is a part, or (b) the title is only a generic term and
needs the name of the corporate body for identification.
Some examples of generic terms often used are: bulletin,
journal, magazine, news, newsletter, proceedings, report,
review, etc. If either (a) or (b) is applicable to the
publication in hand, the main entry is under the issuing
body.

        Main entry under title.

Florida statistical abstract. 1st–   ed.; 1967–
    Gainesville, Bureau of Economic and Business Research,
    University of Florida.

        v. illus., maps. 22 cm. annual.

Card
178

Inspel; international newsletter of special libraries. v. 1–
    Apr. 1966–
    ₍Washington₎

        v. 29 cm. irregular.

    Official organ of the Special Libraries Section of the International
    Federation of Library Associations.
    English, French or Russian.

Card
179

Traffic digest and review.
    ₍Evanston, Ill.₎ Traffic Institute, Northwestern University.

        v. in   illus. 24 cm. monthly.

    Began publication with Apr. 1953 issue, forming a union between
    Traffic digest and Traffic review. Cf. New serial titles, 1950–60.

    1. Traffic safety—Period.   I. Northwestern University, Evanston,
    Ill. Traffic institute.

    HE5601.T58   62–35761

    Library of Congress   ₍1₎

Card
180

Main entry under name of corporate body:

American Water Resources Association.
    Proceedings of the annual meeting. v.1–
1965–
Urbana, Ill.
     v. illus.

Card
181

Fund for Adult Education.
    Report. 1951–
Pasadena, Calif.
     v. illus. 23cm. annual.

Card
182

Indian Library Association.
    Bulletin.
  [New Delhi]

     v. 24 cm. quarterly.

  Began publication in 1965.

Card
183

Special Libraries Association. *Rio Grande Chapter.*
    Bulletin. v. 1–
Apr. 1957–
[n. p.]

    v. in   28 cm. 4 no. a year.

Card
184

Texas Independent Producers & Royalty
    Owners Association
The **TIPRO** reporter.
  [Fort Worth, Tex.]

    v. in   illus. 30 cm. bimonthly.

  Official publication of Texas Independent Producers & Royalty
Owners Association.

Card
185

United States Book Exchange.
    Newsletter.
Washington.

    v. in   29 cm.

  Frequency varies.
  Began publication with Feb. 1949 issue. Cf. Union list of serials.

Card
186

Z690.U7352

67–4578

6-B-2. The North American text has added a second part to
rule 6-B in which an attempt is made to place certain types
of serials under the issuing body regardless of the fact
that it may have a title that is not generic and does not
contain the name of the corporate body that issues it.
Most of these are ones which usually contain only statistics, lists of figures, charts, etc. The British text of
the AA rules does not attempt to make such a distinction
between serials, and no logical reason can be given for
the imposition of this confusing addendum and libraries
would be wise to completely disregard this section and
thereby avoid creating unnecessary complications and
problems.

6-C. Serials by a personal author.

        Any serial by a personal author is entered under
his name.

6-D. Change of title, author, or name of corporate body.

        This part of the rule introduces an excellent im-
provement into the practice of cataloging serials. This
innovation states that a separate entry is to be made each
time a title is changed, irrespective of the fact that the
title may or may not be the main entry. If the serial is
entered under a corporate or personal author and this
changes, then again a separate entry is made for the issues
appearing after the change. With this rule a separate
entry will be made each time a serial changes title or
the name of the issuing body is changed if this is used
as the main entry. References will then connect all the
separate entries for the publication. (For specific de-
tails on the cataloging of serials see Chapter 7, Serials
in the AA rules.) This same principle has been applied to
corporate bodies that change names, cf. rule 68.

WORKS WITH AUTHORSHIP OF MIXED CHARACTER

This group of rules treats those publications whose production involved two or more persons or entities that performed different functions. These rules help the cataloger to determine which contributor to a certain publication is to receive the main entry and which one the added entry. The prime objective is to determine who is most responsible for the work, i.e. who contributed the most important aspect of the publication. In those cases where doubts arise, the rules establish standard policies and preferences for assigning the main and added entries. These guidelines should create more consistency among libraries than under previous sets of cataloging rules.

A work that is based on or related to another publication often needs to have an added entry card made either to help the user of the catalog find a work when the main entry is unknown, or to connect closely related materials with different main entries. The phrase, "Added entry (author-title) under.....", is quite often used to indicate that the cataloger should make an author-title added entry. The glossary includes the term, "Author-title added entry", but no complete card example is given in the text, hence the following example.

```
      Landon, Margaret Dorothea, 1903-
          Anna and the King of Siam.
   Rodgers, Richard, 1902-
          The King and I.  Book and lyrics by
   Oscar Hammerstein.  Music by Richard
   Rodgers.  Based on the novel Anna and          Card
   the King of Siam, by Margaret Landon.           187
   New York, Random House /1951/
          146p.  illus.
```

7. Adapter or original author.

The adaptation or rewriting of a work in a different literary style, such as a paraphrase, an epitome, or a version for children, or in a different literary form, such as a dramatization, novelization or versification, is to be entered under the person who adapted or rewrote the original work. If it is not known who did the adaptation or rewriting the main entry is under the title. (Cf. rule 14)

Showalter, Jean B.
    The donkey ride; a fable adapted by Jean B. Showalter. Illustrated by Tomi Ungerer. ₁1st ed.₎ Garden City, N. Y., Doubleday ₁1967₎

    ₁40₎ p. col. illus. 21 x 27 cm.

    An adaptation of Aesop's fable.

Card 188

The Aeneid of Virgil, retold for
    young children, by A. L. K.
    Based on the translation of
    E. Fairfax Taylor. New York,
    Winston, 1934.
    xii, 176p. illus.

Card 189

Smythe, Percy Ellesmere.
    A complete paraphrase of King Lear, by P. E. Smythe. Sydney, College Press ₁1966₎

    95 p. 19 cm. 70c. Aust.

                                        (Aus 66–1803)

Card 190

Schindel, Morton.
    Alexander and the car with a missing headlight. From a film fantasy created by Peter Fleischmann, with drawings by kindergarten children of Paris. Book adaptation by Morton Schindel. New York, Viking Press ₁1967₎

    1 v. (unpaged) col. illus. 24 x 31 cm.

    ɪ. Fleischmann, Peter. ɪɪ. Title.

    PZ7.S34633Al

    Library of Congress   ₈₎

                        67–20955

Card 191

8. Artist or author of text.

"Artist" is used here in the broad sense of the word and refers to any person whose creative works may be represented pictorially, such as architects, ceramists, designers of fabrics and tapestries, engravers, fashion designers, industrial designers, painters, photographers, sculptors, etc.

8-A. Collaborative work.

A work that is or appears to be a result of the efforts of an artist and the author of the text working jointly should be entered under the one who is named first on the title page, unless the other name is given prominence by wording or typography. In case of doubt, prefer entry under the author of the text. Make an added entry for the one not given the main entry.

Oorthuys, Cas.
    This is London from dawn till night. 114 photos. by Cas Oorthuys. Text by Neville Braybrooke. Oxford, B. Cassirer; distributed by Faber & Faber, London ₁1953₁

    125 p. (chiefly illus.) 19 cm. (Contact photo books of the world)

Card
192

    1. London—Descr.—Views.   I. Braybrooke, Neville, 1923–
        II. Title.

DA684.2.O65   68–43287

Library of Congress   ₁1₁₁

8-B. Illustrated work.

A work for which an artist has provided illustrations is to be entered under the author of the text. The illustrator is given an added entry only if his contribution is considered to be an important feature of the publication.

Godden, Rumer, 1907–
    Impunity Jane; the story of a pocket doll. Illustrated by Adrienne Adams. New York, Viking Press, 1954.

47 p. illus. 21 cm.

Card
193

Andersen, Hans Christian, 1805–1875.
    The nightingale. Translated by Eva Le Gallienne. Designed and illustrated by Nancy Ekholm Burkert. New York, Harper & Row [1965]

32 p. illus. (part col.) 28 cm.

Card
194

    I. Le Gallienne, Eva, 1899–   tr. II. Burkert, Nancy Ekholm, illus. III. Title.

PZ8.A542Ni 31   64—18574

Library of Congress   [6519]

8-C. Illustrations published separately.

Illustrations which were made for a particular work or various works and are later published separately are then entered under the artist. An added entry is made for the work which was illustrated or, if the illustrations were for several works of the same author, then this author should have an added entry.

Blake, William, 1757–1827.
    Blake's Job; William Blake's illustrations of the Book of Job. With an introduction and commentary by S. Foster Damon. Providence, R.I., Brown University Press, 1966.
    ix, 66p.

Card
195

8-D. Reproductions with commentary, etc.

The main entry for a work which consists of reproductions of the works of an artist and text about the artist and/or his work is to be decided by examining the work to see whether the major portion of the book is made up of text or of reproductions of the works of the artist. If the major element is the text, the main entry is under the author, but if the principal portion of the book consists of reproductions and the textual matter is clearly the minor element of the work, the main entry is under the artist.

Stroud, Alice Bab.
 F. Reaugh; Texas longhorn painter, by Alice Bab Stroud and Modena Stroud Dailey. Dallas, Royal Pub. Co. ₁1962₁

 143 p. illus., ports. 21 cm.

 "Prose sketches to accompany the series of paintings by Frank Reaugh entitled, Twenty-four hours with the herd; the text based partly on an earlier sketch by 'Hondo' and written jointly by the painter and by Clyde Walton Hill ... An exact reproduction of an old booklet": p. ₁113₁–₁132₁

 1. Reaugh, Frank, 1860–1945. ɪ. Dailey, Modena Stroud
  ɪɪ. Title: Texas longhorn painter.

ND237.R25S7   927.5   62–52452

Library of Congress ₁2₁

Card 196

Author's text is the more important feature of the publication.

Wynne, David, 1926-
 The sculpture of David Wynne, 1949-1967. Foreword by Yehudi Menuhin. Critical essay by T. S. R. Boase. Photographs by Iain Macmillan. London, Joseph, 1968.
 157p. chiefly illus.

Card 197

Reproductions of the works of the artist form the major element of the publication.

8-E.   Reproductions in exhibition   catalogs.

If reproductions of the works of an artist form the
major element of a catalog of an exhibition of his works,
the publication is to be entered under the artist. An
added entry should be made for the person and/or entity
responsible for the catalog. If the reproductions of the
artist's works are a minor element of the catalog, or if
there is doubt that they do, then the main entry is to be
under the person or entity that is responsible for the
content of the catalog.

Bloom, Hyman, 1913–
 The drawings of Hyman Bloom; an exhibition organized
by the University of Connecticut Museum of Art, 1968.
[Storrs, Conn., 1968]

 1 v. (chiefly illus.) 28 cm.

Card
198

Matisse, Henri, 1869–1954.
 Matisse 1869–1954: a retrospective exhibition at the Hay-
ward Gallery [introductory essay by Lawrence Gowing]
London, Arts Council of Great Britain, 1968.

 172 p. (chiefly illus. (some col.)). 26 cm. 15/-

 Bibliography: p. 45.

(B 68–16508)

Card
199

 i. Gowing, Lawrence. ii. Hayward Gallery. iii. Arts Council
of Great Britain.
     IV. Title.

ND553.M37G6   759.4   68–30337

Library of Congress [2] BOS

9. Biographer/critic or author.

9-A. A publication consisting of a work or a group of
works (e.g. letters, memoirs, diaries, etc.) of an author
which is accompanied by or interwoven with biographical or
critical material by someone else is to be entered under
the person who has contributed the major element of the
publication.

```
Smith, Theodore Clarke, 1870-1960.                         Card
     The life and letters of James Abram Garfield. [Hamden,   200
Conn.] Archon Books, 1968.
     2 v. (ix, 1283 p.)   ports.  24 cm.
```

```
Barrus, Clara, 1864-1931.
     The life and letters of John Burroughs.   New York,
Russell & Russell [1968]

     2 v.  illus., facsims., ports.  23 cm.

     First published in 1925.                               Card
                                                            201




     1. Burroughs, John, 1837-1921.    I. Title.

     PS1226.B27   1968          814'.4  (B)         68-15094

     Library of Congress            [3]
```

9-B. If the person who is responsible for the biographical or critical material is represented as an editor or
compiler, the main entry is under the author of the work
or works included in the publication.

```
Clavering, Sir James, bart., 1680-1748.
     The correspondence of Sir James Clavering; edited and
arranged by H. T. Dickinson.   Gateshead, printed for the
[Surtees] Society by Northumerland P., 1967.

     xvi, 240 p.  geneal. tables.  23 cm.  (The Publications of the Sur-  Card
tees Society, v. 178)  50/-                                    202
                                       (B 68-06007)
     Bibliographical footnotes.



     I. Title.   (Series: Surtees Society, Durham, Eng.  Publications,
v. 178.)

     DA20.S9   vol. 178          942.06'9         68-116102

     Library of Congress            [2]
```

11. Commentator or author.

Works containing both text and commentary need to be examined carefully to determine if the commentator or the author is to be given the main entry. The provisions of this rule help determine if the purpose of the publication in hand is to provide a new edition of the work or a commentary on it. If the purpose is to provide a new edition the main entry is under the author, but if the purpose is to furnish a commentary on the work then the main entry is made under the commentator. Guidelines to be used in determining the purpose of the publication in hand are: (1) a statement in the prefatory material that would indicate whether the purpose was to provide an edition or a commentary, (2) the proportions of the book devoted to the text and the commentary, (3) the kind of type used made either the text or the commentary typographically subordinate to the other one, (4) the text might be so broken up by commentary that it cannot be read conveniently by itself, thereby making it subordinate to the commentary.

Tertullian.
    Treatise on the resurrection. De resurrectione carnis liber. The text edited with an introd., translation, and commentary by Ernest Evans. London, S. P. C. K., 1960.

    xxvi, 361 p. 22 cm.

Card 203

Slocum, Joshua, *b.* 1844.
    Sailing alone around the world and Voyage of the Liberdade. Edited and with commentaries by Walter Magnes Teller. New York, Collier Books [1962, ᶜ1958]

    382 p. illus. 18 cm. (Collier books, AS252)

    "Originally appeared as part of a collection entitled The voyages of Joshua Slocum."

Card 204

Frost, Robert, 1874–1963.
    The road not taken; an introduction to Robert Frost. A selection of Robert Frost's poems with a biographical pref. and running commentary by Louis Untermeyer. Illus. by John O'Hara Cosgrave II. New York, Holt [1951]

    xxxvii, 282 p. illus. 21 cm.

    An enlargement of the author's Come in.

    I. Untermeyer, Louis, 1885–   ed. II. Title.

    PS3511.R94A6 1951   811.5   51—9831

    Library of Congress   [a66r59h²½]

Card 205

Stanislavsky, Constantin, 1863-1938.
    Stanislavsky produces Othello.
Translated from the Russian by Dr.
Helen Nowak. London, Geoffrey Bles,
1948.
    244p.

Card
206

Sisson, Charles Jasper, 1885-
    New readings in Shakespeare. London, Dawsons of Pall
Mall, 1961.

    2 v. facsims. 19 cm.

    CONTENTS.—v. 1. Introduction. The comedies. The poems.—v. 2.
The histories. The tragedies.

Card
207

    1. Shakespeare, William—Criticism, Textual.   I. Title.

PR3071.S48   1961   822.33   62-697

    Library of Congress   [1]

14.   Reviser or original author.

        Revisions, enlargements, abridgments, condensations
and other such variations on the original text made by
someone other than the author are to be entered under the
original author with an added entry for the other person.
However, when a work has been so changed that it can no
longer be attributed to the original author then the person
who created the new edition will receive the main entry
and an author-title added entry is made for the earlier work.

        A comparison of rules 7 and 14 shows that if the
new edition of a work is in the same literary form and style
and at the same time is still indentifiable as the work of
the original author, then the main entry remains under the
original author. If the original work has been rewritten
in another literary form or style, of if the new edition is
obviously no longer the work of the original author then the
person responsible for the new edition is given the main
entry.

According to the ALA rules paraphrases, free translations, epitomes, and outlines were generally entered under the original author, but with the AA rules it is considered that these adaptations are changed to such an extent that the main entry should be under the person who rewrote the work and not under the original author.

Dickens, Charles, 1812-1870.
A tale of two cities. Abridged and edited with notes and introduction by Margaret Coult. New York, University Pub. Co., 1904.
xvi, 238p.

Card 208

Wilmore, Albert, 1862?-1932.
The groundwork of modern geography. 5th ed., revised by Ethel R. Payne. London, Bell, 1961.
412p. illus.

Card 209

McColvin, Lionel Roy, 1896–
Music libraries, including a comprehensive bibliography of music literature and a select bibliography of music scores published since 1957, by Lionel Roy McColvin and Harold Reeves. Completely re-written, rev. and extended by Jack Dove. ₍London₎ A. Deutsch ₍1965₎

2 v. illus. 22 cm. (A Grafton book)

Card 210

Sorenson, Roy, 1900–
Step by step in better board and committee work. Drawn from Roy Sorenson's How to be a board or committee member. Programed by William C. Tuck. New York, Association Press ₍1962₎

119 p. 22 cm. (An Association Press programed instruction book)

Card 211

1. Associations, institutions, etc. 2. Social service. ɪ. Tuck, William C. ɪɪ. Title.

HS35.S62   1962   301.1583   62-16869 ‡

Library of Congress   ₍5₎

15. Translator or author.

15-A. A translation of a work is to be entered under the author of the original work. However, if the translation involves adaptation or is described as a "free" translation, it should be treated according to the provisions of rule 7. Make an added entry under the translator only if the translation is in verse or if the work has been translated into the same language by many different translators.

Anckarsvärd, Karin, 1918–
    Springtime for Eva. Translated from the Swedish by Annabelle MacMillan. ₁1st American ed.₎ New York, Harcourt, Brace ₁1961₎

    157 p. 21 cm.

    Translation of Liten roman om Eva.

Card
212

    ɪ. Title.

PZ7.A5187Sp   61–12340 ‡

Library of Congress   ₁10₎

15-B. A collection of translations of works by different authors should be treated according to the provisions of rule 5.

Borski, Lucia Merecka, comp.
    The jolly tailor, and other fairy tales. Translated from the Polish by Lucia Merecka Borski and Kate B. Miller. Illustrated by Kazimir Klepacki. New York, Longmans, Green, 1928.
    156p. illus.

Card
213

---

16. Writer or ·nominal writer.

A work which has been narrated or dictated to someone who later writes it up (e.g. ghostwriter) and is later presented as a work of the narrator is entered under the name of the person who dictated or narrated the material. The writer is given an added entry.

Holloway, Stanley.
   Wiv a little bit o' luck; the life story of Stanley Holloway, as told to Dick Richards. New York, Stein and Day ₁1967₎

   223 p. illus., ports. 22 cm.

Card
214

   1. Actors—Correspondence, reminiscences, etc.   ɪ. Richards, Dick.
ɪɪ. Title.

PN2598.H63A3   1967b   790.2′0924   67–25621

Library of Congress   ₍5₎

---

17. Corporate author or personal author.

It is not an uncommon work that might require a close examination in order to determine its purpose, contents and the kind of work it is, before it can be decided if its authorship should be attributed to a person or to a corporate body. Some typical examples of entities which fall under the definition of a corporate body are associations, institutions, business firms, non-profit enterprises, governments, specific agencies of government, conferences, expeditions and churches.

17-A. Works of corporate authorship.

Works which should be entered under corporate authorship are: (a) those written by an official or employee of the corporate body which are official records and reports, and statements, studies and other writings concerning the policies, operations or management of the body, (b) publications that describe the body, its functions, procedures, facilities, resources, etc., or an inventory, catalog, directory of personnel, list of members, etc., (c) single reports of scholarly or scientific research written by four or more officials or employees of which no one is represented as the principal author.

Hurty-Peck & Company. *Library.*
    A bibliography of books and booklets on beverages, their history and manufacture. Also contains a reasonably complete list of all other known titles on the same subject which are not now in the Hurty-Peck Library. Compiled by A. W. Noling. Indianapolis, Hurty-Peck [1961]

    55 p. illus., port. 23 cm.

Card 215

John Crerar Library.
    A list of books on the history of science, January, 1911. Prepared by Aksel G. S. Josephson, cataloguer. Chicago, Printed by order of the Board of Directors, 1911. New York, Kraus Reprint Corp., 1966.

    297 p. 27 cm.

Card 216

Rhode Island. *Dept. of Education.*
    Financing tomorrow's schools today; the story of Rhode Island's school finance program, by E. Gil Boyer, assistant commissioner. [Providence, 1961]

    60 p. illus. 23 cm.

Card 217

    1. Education—Rhode Island—Finance.   I. Boyer, E. Gil. II. Title.

LB2826.R4A53   379.1109745   61–62986 ‡

Library of Congress   [1]

17-B. Works not of corporate authorship.

    Works which should be entered under personal authorship are: (a) formal histories of the corporate body, (b) reports and studies by consultants engaged for that specific purpose, (c) single reports of scholarly or scientific research written by no more than three officials or employees, (d) any work that does not fit any of the categories for corporate authorship or if there is doubt as to whether it would, is to be entered under the appropriate heading under which it would be entered if no corporate body were involved.

Stageman, Anne.
Hospital-nursing home relationship; selected references annotated. Prepared by Anne Stageman [and] Anna Mae Baney. Washington, U. S. Dept. of Health, Education, and Welfare, Public Health Service, Division of Hospital and Medical Facilities, Program Evaluation and Reports Branch [1962]
iv, 25 p. 28 cm. (Hospital and medical facilities series (under the Hill-Burton program) : Bibliography)
Public Health Service publication no. 930–G–2.

Card
218

Stafford, Walter H
Artificial earth satellites and successful solar probes, 1957–1960, by Walter H. Stafford and Robert M. Croft. Washington, National Aeronautics and Space Administration. 1961.

602 p. illus. 26 cm. ([U. S.] National Aeronautics and Space Administration. Technical note D–601)

Includes bibliography.

1. Artificial satellites. 2. Artificial satellites—Sun.   I. Croft, Robert M.   II. Title.

TL521.A3525   D–601   629.435   61–61024 ‡

Card
219

Library of Congress   [5]

17-C.   Works by chiefs of state, heads of governments, etc.

17-C-1.   Official communications.

An official communication, such as a message to a legislature or governing body, a proclamation or an executive order, which is issued by a chief of state, a head of government, or a head of an international intergovernmental body is to be entered under the corporate heading for the office held by the person who issued the communication. However, in case of doubt as to the official character of a communication, enter it under the provisions of rule 17-C-2.

```
    U. S. President, 1961-1963 (Kennedy)
       John Fitzgerald Kennedy's
    Thanksgiving proclamation for
    1963.  Washington, U.S. Govt.          Card
    Print. Off., 1964.                     220
       4p.
```

17-C-2. Other speeches and writings.

Enter any other speech or writing of such a person according to the general rules for personal authorship.

```
    Nixon, Richard Milhous, 1913-
       Inaugural address of Richard
    Milhous Nixon, President of the
    United States, delivered at the        Card
    Capitol, Washington, D.C., January     221
    20, 1969.  Washington, U.S. Govt.
    Print. Off., 1969.
       ii, 5p.
```

18.   Corporate body or subordinate unit.

18-A.   A work which is specifically and prominently attributed to a subordinate unit of a corporate body is entered
under the heading for the subordinate unit according to the
appropriate rule in the chapter on headings for corporate
bodies.   If the subordinate unit simply acts as the information or publication agent for the parent body   an ex-
planatory reference is made from the heading for the subordinate unit.

American Library Association. *Personnel Publications Committee.*
   Personnel organization and procedure; a manual suggested for use in public libraries. 2d ed. Chicago, American Library Association, 1968.
   59 p. forms. 28 cm.

Card
222

American Library Association. *Division of Cataloging and Classification.*
   A. I. A. cataloging rules for author and title entries.
2d ed., edited by Clara Beetle. Chicago, American Library
Assn., 1949.
   xxi, 265 p. 27 cm.

Card
223

American Management Association. *Packaging Division.*
   The potential of packaging: the need for better management, new materials for packaging, advances in packaging
machinery, implications for marketing, shipping and distributing [and] European packaging trends. [New York,
1963]
   51 p. 29 cm. ([American Management Association] Management
bulletin 31)

   Cover title.

   1. Packaging.   I. Title   (Series)

   HF5770.A655   658.564   63–24120

   Library of Congress   [8]

Card
224

18-B.   If the responsibility of the subordinate unit for
preparing the work is not stated prominently or if the
subordinate unit cannot be identified, enter the work
under the parent body with no mention of a subordinate
unit.

19. Related works.

This rule for related works excludes adaptations, revisions, and translations which are covered by rules 7, 14 and 15. Included here are: continuations, supplements, indexes, concordances, manuals, sequels, scenarios, choreographies, librettos, subseries, special numbers of serials, collections of extracts from serials, etc.

A work with a title that is indistinctive and dependent on the title of another work is entered under the same author and/or title (if the main entry is under the title) as the work to which it is related if it is one of the following types: (a) indexes, teacher's manuals, and other auxiliary works which must be used in connection with one specific edition of the principal work, (b) supplements that are continuations of the main work, except for a supplement by a different author that takes the form of an independent work, and (c) subseries and serial supplements of serial publications. Entries for publications in the first two categories are normally, and those of the third group may be, made part of the cataloging of the works to which they are related.

School Mathematics Study Group.
    Analytic geometry. Student's text. Rev. ed.
Prepared by H. Glenn Ayre ₁and others₁   New
Haven, Yale University Press, 1965.
    577 p. illus.
    "Unit no. 64."
—— ——Teacher's commentary. Rev. ed. Prepared by H. Glenn Ayre ₁and others₁   New
Haven, Yale University Press, 1965.
    494 p.
    "Unit no. 65."

Card 225

Morgan, Dale Lowell, 1914–
    Life in America: the West. Picture maps by Janet Croninger, Charles Vanderwoud, and Charles McMullin. Grand Rapids, Fideler Co. ₁1952₁

    160 p. illus. 28 cm. ("Life in America" books)

—— ——— Unit of teaching pictures. ₁Grand Rapids, Informative Classroom Picture Publishers, 1952₁

    30 l., 48 plates (in portfolio) 30 cm. (Informative classroom picture series. Life in America library)
                 F591.M86p

    1. The West.   I. Title.

F591.M86   917.8   52—5954 ‡

    Library of Congress   ₁59r55f²₁

Card 226

Sharp, Alice M
    The Bible for all the world; a vacation church
school text (10 sessions). ₁Rev. ed.₁
Philadelphia, Judson Press ₁1956₁
    104 p. 26 cm. (Judson Series, Junior de-
partment)
    ——Pupil's work sheets for use with The Bible
for all the world. Philadelphia, Judson Press,
1956.
    11 sheets in envelope. illus. 29 cm.
    1.Bible—Hist.   I. Title.

Card
227

Special Inter-American Conference. 2d, Rio de
Janeiro, 1965.
    Actas y documentos (versión preliminar)
Washington, Unión Panamericana, 1965.
    4 v. 28 cm. (OEA/ser. E/XIII. 3 (español))
    —— ——. ₁Suplemento: documentos omitidos₁
Washington, Unión Panamericana, 1965.
    1 v. (various pagings) 28 cm.

Card
228

International Conference on Cloud Physics, *Tokyo and*
Sapporo, 1965.
    Proceedings. ₁Tokyo? 1965₁
    xi, 524 p. illus. 26 cm.
    Organized by the Meteorological Society of Japan. Sponsored by
    the International Association of Meteorology and Atmospheric
    Physics.
    Includes bibliographies.
    —— ———— Supplement. ₁Tokyo? 1965₁
    iv, 185 p. illus. 26 cm.
    Includes bibliographies.
                         QC921.5.I 55 1965 Suppl.
    1. Cloud physics—Congresses.   I. Nihon Kishogakkai. II. Inter-
    national Association of Meteorology and Atmospheric Physics.

QC921.5.I 55   1965   67–4484

Library of Congress   ₁3₁

Card
229

    All other related works are to be entered according
to the general rules. Make an author-title or a title
added entry for the work to which it is related, as appropriate.

33. Added entries.

Thoughout the rules it is often indicated when an added entry is to be made in a specific situation, but only under the provisions of the fourteen sections of this rule are to be found definite guidelines for making added entries of all types, and for practically every situation.

The only section of this rule that contains very precise examples is section "J." which covers added entries for persons identified cryptically. The other sections only indicate in which cases the added entries are to be made, but no examples with the proper designations of function are given. As mentioned in the introduction to this chapter the designations of function should be limited to: "comp.", "ed.", "illus." and "tr.". The appropriate one is added at the end of the heading to indicate the function performed. Never more than one is used in a single added entry and they are used only with personal names and never with corporate names.

Whenever the cataloger feels that an added entry is needed and no specific rule provides for it in that particular case, sections "H. Other related persons and bodies." and "L. Other relationships." allow him to make any that are needed in special situations.

Carlyle, Alexander, 1797-1876.
Carlyle, Thomas, 1795-1881.
    The letters of Thomas Carlyle to his brother Alexander, with related family letters. Edited by Edwin W. Marrs, Jr. Cambridge, Belknap Press of Harvard University Press, 1968.

    xiii, 830 p. illus., geneal. tables, map, ports. 25 cm. $15.00
    Bibliography: p. [797]-799.

Card 230

    I. Carlyle, Alexander, 1797-1876. II. Marrs, Edwin W., ed. III. Title.

PR4433.A5C23   826'.8   68-21978

Library of Congress   [3]   BOS

In cataloging the works of prolific authors, or any author that is widely published in many editions, translations, etc. many libraries will find that one reference card could take the place of several added entry cards. (Cf. rule 126.)

```
 Joesten, Joachim, 1907-
    Denmark's day of doom.


       For all editions, translations,            Author-Title
    selections, commentaries, and other           Reference Card
    publications related to this work see:

 Joesten, Joachim, 1907-                               Card
    Rats in the larder.                                231
```

```
       Denmark's day of doom
  Joesten, Joachim

          For all editions, translations,          Title-Author
       selections, commentaries, and other          Reference Card
       publications related to this work see:

  Joesten, Joachim, 1907-                               Card
     Rats in the larder.                                232
```

The knight's tale
Chaucer, Geoffrey

    For all editions, translations,
selections, commentaries, and other
publications related to this work see:

Chaucer, Geoffrey, d.1400
    Canterbury tales. The knight's tale.

Title-Author
Reference Card

Card
233

The pearl
Steinbeck, John

    For all editions, translations,
selections, commentaries, and other
publications related to this work see:

Steinbeck, John, 1902-1968
    The pearl.

Title-Author
Reference Card

Card
234

Steinbeck, John, 1902-1968
    The pearl.
Eliot, George, 1819-1880
    Silas Marner, by George Eliot. The pearl,
by John Steinbeck. Edited by Jay E. Greene.
New York, Noble and Noble [1953]
    451p. illus. 20cm.

Analytical
Author-Title
Added Entry Card

Card
235

CHAPTER III

UNIFORM TITLES -- Rules 100-107

The term "uniform title" has been selected as the standard expression for "the particular title by which a work that has appeared under varying titles is to be identified for cataloging purposes", as it is stated in the AA rules. This term is not new, but previously it was usually used only in reference to classical literary works, such as anonymous classics and sacred scriptures. In the AA rules its meaning and use have been expanded to include: (a) the "conventional titles" which have been used for many years in the cataloging of music, (b) the "filing titles" which the Library of Congress has used to file cards in its own catalogs, (c) common titles used as main entries for anonymous works (See Appendix I), and (d) any common or standard title assigned to collections, translations, and any other editions of an author's works in order to facilitate their logical grouping and arrangement in the card catalog.

The introduction of uniform titles into the cataloging practices of all libraries would create a better organization of many authors' works in the catalog. It is extremely unfortunate that the Library of Congress has not felt it necessary to introduce this practice into its cataloging, except in a few cases where it was already done before the publication of the AA rules. But, regardless of this fact, most libraries will find that the application of these rules on uniform titles will not only facilitate the use of the catalog, but will also enhance the effectiveness of searches for works under a single main entry.

The purpose of these rules is to encompass and unify all previous practices in the assigning and use of uniform titles, and at the same time provide for uniform titles to be used for any type of material wherever their use would facilitate its organization and arrangement in the catalog.

100. Basic rules.

These basic rules point out the importance of selecting one title as the uniform title under which all editions, translations, etc., of a work will be cataloged. There are two ways in which the uniform titles are used: (1) as a heading for works entered title, and (2) as a bracketed title interposed between the transcribed title and the main entry, which must be either personal or corporate authorship.

Three little pigs.
   The three little pigs. Illustrated by Bonnie & Bill Rutherford and Eulalie. New York, Platt & Munk ₁1961₁

   28 p. illus. 25 cm. (An Early fun-to-read classic)

Card 236

The three bears.
   The three bears and Goldilocks. Edited by Nova Nestrick. Illustrated by Barbara Remington. New York, Platt & Munk ₁1962₁

   28 p. illus. 24 cm. (An Early fun-to-read classic)

Card 237

Mother Goose.
   The real Mother Goose. Chicago, Rand, McNally & co. ₁ᶜ1961₁

   ₁132₁ p. col. front., col. illus. 31 x 25½ cm.

   Illustrated t.-p. and lining-papers.
   On cover: With pictures by Blanche Fisher Wright.

Card 238

Arabian nights.
   The Arabian nights, their best-known tales, ed. by Kate Douglas Wiggin and Nora A. Smith, illustrated by Maxfield Parrish. New York, C. Scribner's sons, 1909.

   xii, 339 p. 12 col. pl. 24 cm.

   Illustrated t.-p. and end-papers.
   Each plate accompanied by guard sheet with descriptive letterpress.

   I. Wiggin, Kate Douglas   1856–1923, ed. II. Smith, Nora
   Archibald   III. Parrish, Maxfield, 1870–   illus. IV. Title.

   PZ8.A85 25   9—28132

   Library of Congress   ₁6Go²½₁

Card 239

Card
240

Card
241

    If an edition of a work is published under the same
title (either with or without a subtitle) as that chosen
for the uniform title, there is no need to interpose a
title between the main entry and the transcribed title.
However, there are times when the addition of another element is required for the organization of the cards in the
catalog, or when it is impossible to use punctuation to
set apart from the rest of the transcribed title and in
these cases it will be necessary to interpose the appropriate uniform title. (Cf. rules 105, 106 and 107)

Swift, Jonathan, 1667-1745.
/Gulliver's travels7
Gulliver's travels into several
remote nations of the world, including
the voyages to Lilliput, Brobdingnag,
Laputa, Balnibarbi, Luggnag, Glubbdub-
drib, and Japan. Illustrated with 8
colour plates and line drawings by
Arthur Rackham. London, Dent; New
York, Dutton /1952/
xiii, 210p. illus.

Card
242

Hawthorne, Nathaniel, 1804-1864.
The scarlet letter, a romance. With an introd., a note on
the text, a bibliography, and an annotated chronology, prepared by Hyatt H. Waggoner and George Monteiro. San
Francisco, Chandler Pub. Co. [1968]

lx, 4, iv, 322 p. 19 cm. (Chandler facsimile editions in American
literature)

Text is a facsimile of the first edition published in 1850.
Bibliography : p. liv-lviii.

Card
243

Shakespeare, William, 1564-1616
Hamlet. Edited, introduced, and with facing-page notes
by Edmund Fuller. [New York, Dell Pub. Co., 1967, °1966]

407, [4] p. port. 18 cm. (Invitation to Shakespeare)

The Laurel-leaf library.
Bibliography : p. [411]

Card
244

Shakespeare, William, 1564-1616.

[Hamlet. German]

Hamlet, Prinz von Dänemark. Übersetzt von Theodor
Fontane. (Im Auftrag der Universitätsbibliothek der
Humboldt-Universität zu Berlin hrsg. von Joachim Krue-
ger.) Berlin, Weimar, Aufbau-Verlag, 1966.

163 p. 22 cm. DM 7.80

(GDNB 66-A51-315)

r. Fontane, Theodor, 1819-1898, tr. II. Title.

PR2807.A5F6   67-84141

Library of Congress   [2]

Card
245

CHOICE AND FORM OF TITLE.

101. Works written after 1500.

101-A. The general rule for choosing the uniform titles is that the title of the original edition of a work written after 1500 should be preferred. An alternative to this rule should be made for those libraries that do not generally collect works in foreign languages and would not normally want to use uniform titles in languages unknown to their clienteles.

Alternative rule:
101-A. Except as qualified by rules 101-B, 101-C and 101-D, prefer the uniform title in English for all editions (including those in the original language) and translations of a work written after 1500. If the English translation of a work has retained the title in the original language, or is better known by the title in the original language, use this title as the uniform title. The title of the original edition should be used for those publications in foreign languages which have never been translated into English. (Cf. Alternative rules for 102-A and 105-A)

102. Works written before 1501.

The same principle of preferring the title in the original language of a work written after 1500 applies to those written before 1501. However, exceptions are made for classical Greek works (q.v. Rule 102-B) and anonymous works not written in the Roman alphabet (q.v. Rule 102-C-2) which may have the uniform titles in English.

An alternative to this rule is needed so that it conforms to the alternative for Rule 101-A.

Alternative rule:

102-A. Prefer the uniform title in English by which a work written before 1501 has become identified in reference sources. If there is no title in English, or evidence in reference sources is insufficient or inconclusive, prefer the title most frequently used in modern editions, early editions or manuscript copies, in the order given. (Cf. Alternative rules for 101-A and 105-A)

105. <u>Translations</u>.

This rule for translations is very important and practical for libraries that have research collections in which content and subject matter take precedence over the language in which the book is published. But, for other libraries, such as public, school, and possibly the junior and community college libraries, which do not generally collect works in foreign languages and whose clientele would not usually be interested in publications in foreign languages the following alternative would be quite useful.

Alternative rule:

105-A. Use a uniform title in English for all editions (including those in the original language) and translations of a work of which there exists an English translation. If the work in hand is not in English add after the uniform title the name of the language in which it is written, even if it is the original language. If the language is an early form of a modern language designate its form in parentheses after the name of the modern language, e.g. French (Old French). (Cf. Alternative rules for 101-A and 102-A)

For those libraries whose collections are almost entirely in English the use of the alternatives to rules 101-A, 102-A and 105-A will prove to be the most logical and practical. The following card examples show the use of uniform titles for translations. Cards 246-255 show the use of the original title as the uniform title according to the AA rules 100-105. The next ten cards, numbers 256-265, for the same 10 books illustrate the use of the alternative rules which are especially designed for libraries whose collections are almost entirely in English.

Ibsen, Henrik, 1828-1906
    Et dukkehjem; et drama i tre akter af
H. Ibsen. Oslo, Gyldendal, 1937.
    184p.

Card
246

Ibsen, Henrik, 1828-1906
    [Et dukkehjem. English]
    A doll's house. Newly translated from
the Norwegian by Robert Sharp. New York,
Putnam, 1918.
    153p.

Card
247

Ibsen, Henrik, 1828-1906
    [Et dukkehjem. English]
    Nora; or A doll's house. Translated into
English by Miles Dawson. Toronto, Dent, 1915.
    135p.

Card
248

Ibsen, Henrik, 1828-1906
    [Et dukkehjem. English]
    Nora, and Ghosts; two plays by H. Ibsen.
New York, Modern Library, 1935.
    284p.

Card
249

Ibsen, Henrik, 1828-1906
    [Et dukkehjem. Spanish]
    La casa de muñecas; un drama. Traducido
al español por Juan Fernandez. Madrid,
Aguilar, 1929.
    183p.

Card
250

Hitler, Adolf, 1889-1945
   Mein Kampf. Zwei bände in einem band.
München, Zentralverlag, 1938.
   ix, 1003p.

Card
251

Hitler, Adolf, 1889-1945
   [Mein Kampf. English]
   Mein Kampf. The first complete and
unexpurgated edition published in English.
New York, Stackpole, 1939.
   781p.

Card
252

Hitler, Adolf, 1889-1945
   [Mein Kampf. English]
   My battle. Complete and unabridged.
New York, Reynal & Hitchcock, 1940.
   xxv, 781 p.

Card
253

Hitler, Adolf, 1889-1945
   [Mein Kampf. English]
   My struggle. Translated into English by
Ralph Manheim. Boston, Houghton, Mifflin, 1943.
   xix, 694p.

Card
254

Hitler, Adolf, 1889-1945
   [Mein Kampf. Spanish]
   Mi lucha. Traducción directa del alemán.
Barcelona, Casa Editorial Araluce, 1935.
   367p.

Card
255

Ibsen, Henrik, 1828-1906
   A doll's House. Newly translated from
the Norwegian by Robert Sharp. New York,
Putnam, 1918.
   153p.

Card
256

Ibsen, Henrik, 1828-1906
   [A doll's house]
   Nora; or A doll's house. Translated into
English by Miles Dawson. Toronto, Dent, 1915.
   135p.

Card
257

Ibsen, Henrik, 1828-1906
   [A doll's house].
   Nora, and Ghosts; two plays by H. Ibsen.
New York, Modern Library, 1935.
   284p.

Card
258

Ibsen, Henrik, 1828-1906
   [A doll's house. Norwegian]
   Et dukkehjem; et drama i tre akter af
H. Ibsen. Oslo, Gyldendal, 1937.
   184p.

Card
259

Ibsen, Henrik, 1828-1906
   [A doll's house. Spanish]
   La casa de muñecas; un drama. Traducido
al español por Juan Fernandez. Madrid,
Aguilar, 1929.
   183p.

Card
260

Hitler, Adolf, 1889-1945
  Mein Kampf. The first complete and
unexpurgated edition published in English.
New York, Stackpole, 1939.
  781p.

Card
261

Hitler, Adolf, 1889-1945
  [Mein Kampf]
  My battle. Complete and unabridged.
New York, Reynal & Hitchcock, 1940.
  xxv, 781p.

Card
262

Hitler, Adolf, 1889-1945
  [Mein Kampf]
  My struggle. Translated into English by
Ralph Manheim. Boston, Houghton, Mifflin, 1943.
  xix, 694p.

Card
263

Hitler, Adolf, 1889-1945
  [Mein Kampf. German]
  Mein Kampf. Zwei bände in einem band.
Munchen, Zentralverlag, 1938.
  ix, 1003p.

Card
264

Hitler, Adolf, 1889-1945
  [Mein Kampf. Spanish]
  Mi lucha. Traducción directa del alemán.
Barcelona, Casa Editorial Araluce, 1935.
  367p.

Card
265

106. Parts of a work.

106-A. Single parts.

Parts of works are sometimes published separately and in these cases the cataloger must decide if the separately published part should be treated as an independent work or as a subheading under the uniform title of the whole work.

Use the title or designation of the part as a subheading of the uniform title of the whole work if the part has no distinct title or is normally considered as a subordinate part of the whole work.

Longfellow, Henry Wadsworth, 1807-1882.
    [Hiawatha. 3. Hiawatha's childhood]
Hiawatha's childhood, from "The song of
Hiawatha", by Henry Wadsworth Longfellow.
Illustrated by Herbert Morton Stoops.
Garden City, N.Y., Garden City Publishing
Company [c1941]
    15p. 27cm.

Card 266

Shakespeare, William, 1564-1616.

    [Henry VI. Part 1]

    The first part of King Henry the Sixth. **Edited by**
David Bevington. Baltimore, Penguin Books [1966]

    131 p. 18 cm. (The Pelican Shakespeare, AB34)

Card 267

Shakespeare, William, 1564-1616.
    [Henry VI. Part 2]

    The second and third parts of King Henry the Sixth.
Edited by Robert K. Turner, Jr. and George Walton Williams. Baltimore, Penguin Books [1967]

    273 p. 18 cm. (The Pelican Shakespeare, AB35)

    1. Henry VI, King of England, 1421-1471—Drama. I. Turner,
Robert K., ed. II. Williams, George Walton, 1922- ed. III. Title.

PR2815.A2T8   822'.3'3   66-13630

Library of Congress   [5]

Card 268

106-B. Several parts.

When two parts taken from a single work are published together the same criteria are applied for deciding
if the first of the two parts should be entered as an independent work, or as a subheading under the uniform title
of the whole work. An author-title added entry is made
for the second part in the same form as that decided upon
for the first part.

A publication that is made up of three or more parts
of a work, or of various extracts or quotations from it
should be entered under the uniform title for the whole work
followed by the subheading, "Selections".

Swift, Jonathan, 1667-1745.
    [Gulliver's travels. A voyage to Lilliput]
    Gulliver's travels, the voyages to Lilliput
and Brobdingnag. Edited by Charles Robert
Gaston. New York, American Book Co., 1914.
    152p. 17cm.

Card
269

    Swift, Jonathan, 1667-1745.
        Gulliver's travels. A voyage to Brobdingnag
Swift, Jonathan, 1667-1745.
    [Gulliver's travels. A voyage to Lilliput]
    Gulliver's travels, the voyages to Lilliput
and Brobdingnag. Edited by Charles Robert
Gaston. New York, American Book Co., 1914.
    152p. 17cm.

Card
270

Irving, Washington, 1783-1859.

    [The sketch book. Selections]

    The legend of Sleepy Hollow, Little Britain & The spec-
tre bridegroom from The sketch book. Ann Arbor, University Microfilms, 1966.

    xi, 176 p. illus. 21 cm. (A **Legacy** library facsimile)

    Facsimile of the edition published by Sampson, Low, London, ca.
1880, with original title reading: Little Britain, together with The
spectre bridegroom & A legend of Sleepy Hollow. Illustrated by
Chas. O. Murray.

    ı. Title. ıı. Title: Little Britain. ııı. Title: The spectre bride-
groom.

PS2052.S3 1880a   67-347

Library of Congress   ₍3₎

Card
271

Use the title of a part of a whole as a uniform
title if it has a distinct title and not just a numerical
designation, and is a unit of a loosely organized series,
trilogy, collection, etc., or if it has a well established
title of its own that is not usually regarded as a subordinate part of the whole work.

```
     Galsworthy, John, 1867-1933.
        To let.  London, W. Heinemann, 1922.
        viii, 312p.  18cm.                        Card
                                                  272
        "Sequel to Awakening and completes
     The Forsyte saga."
```

A well known poem, short story, essay or other such
work which originally appeared as a part of a whole work
and later was published as a separate work under its own
title by which it is cited in reference sources should be
entered under its own title and not as a subheading under
the uniform title established for the work from which it
was taken.

```
     Hawthorne, Nathaniel, 1804-1864.
        Golden fleece, from the Tanglewood tales,
     by Nathaniel Hawthorne.  Drawings by Helen
     Noel.  Chicago, Black Cat Press, 1936.         Card
        57p.  illus.  24cm.                          273
```

Works made up of parts which might be published
separately vary greatly and many will need a close examination of the general nature of the larger work, the close-
ness of the interconnection of its parts, and the nature
of the separately published part before a final decision
can be reached.

107. <u>Collected editions, etc.</u>

There is no doubt that the application of the provisions of this rule will do more than any other one rule
to improve the arrangement of a prolific author's works in
the catalog. The interpolation of these generic collective
titles before the transcribed title page information will
group similar writings of an author in such a way that
searching in the catalog is greatly facilitated.

The following uniform titles are always used in
English (or the official language of the locale where the
library is located), and only for collections compiled
from the works of a single author. No language is indicated after the title if the publication is in the same
language as that chosen for establishing the uniform titles
of individual works by the same author. In all other cases
the name of the language follows the collective uniform title.

107-A. The single word "Works" used as a collective title
for complete or purportedly complete editions of
an author's writings will place all editions of his
complete works together in the catalog.

Swinburne, Algernon Charles, 1837–1909.
　　[Works]
　　The complete works of Algernon Charles Swinburne.
Edited by Sir Edmund Gosse and Thomas James Wise.
New York, Russell & Russell [1968]

　　20 v. 23 cm.
　　Reprint of the Bonchurch edition, first published in 1925.
　　CONTENTS.—v. 1–6. Poetical works.—v. 7–10. Tragedies.—v. 11–17.
Prose works.—v. 18. Letters.—v. 19. The life of Algernon Charles
Swinburne, by Sir E. Gosse.—v. 20. A bibliography of the writings
in prose and verse of Algernon Charles Swinburne, by T. J. Wise.

　　1. Swinburne, Algernon Charles, 1837–1909. 2. Swinburne, Algernon Charles, 1837–1909—Bibl.　　I. Gosse, Sir Edmund William,
1849–1928, ed.　II. Wise, Thomas James, 1859–1937, ed.　III. Title.

　　[PR5500]　　　　　　　828'.8'09　　　　68–15164/CD
Printed for Card Div.
Library of Congress　　　　[3]

Card
274

107-B. The use of "Selected works" will vary depending on
the literary writings of each author. For those
authors who have written in only one literary form,
or almost exclusively in one form, the uniform title
"Selected works" will be assigned to collections of
his works in that form which are not "complete works".
This same uniform title is also used for collections
of the writings of an author in various literary
forms.

Ibsen, Henrik, 1828-1906.
  [Selected works]
  The league of youth; A doll's house;
The lady from the sea. Translated by
Peter Watts. Baltimore, Penguin [c1965]
  335p. 19cm.

Card
275

Kipling, Rudyard, 1865-1936.

  [Selected works]

  The best of Kipling. Garden City, N. Y., N. Doubleday,
1968.

    669 p. illus. 22 cm.

    CONTENTS. — Kim. — Captains courageous. — Without benefit of
clergy.—They.—The man who would be king.—Barrack-room bal-
lads.—The light that failed.

  I. Title.

  PZ3.K629Bg   68–622

  Library of Congress   [5]

Card
276

107-C. The term "Selections" is not only used as a subheading after the uniform title for three or more parts
of a single work or of various extracts from it
(q.v. rule 106-B-3), but also for publications that
consist of parts, extracts, quotations, etc. from
various works of an author.

"Selected works" is distinguished from "Selections" in that it is used only for works in their entirety, irrespective of the fact that they be short stories, poems, essays, etc., and "Selections" is only for excerpts, passages, citations, etc. taken from several works.

Shakespeare, William, 1564–1616.
   [Selections]
    Shakespeare's best: memorable words from the great poems and plays. With original woodcuts by Don Dubowski. Edited by David Curtis. ₍Kansas City, Mo.₎ Hallmark Editions ₍1967₎

      62 p. Illus. (part col.) 20 cm.

    I. Curtis, David L., ed. II. Title.

PR2768.C8   822'.3'3   67–17901

Library of Congress   ₍5₎

Card 277

107-D. If there are also complete or purportedly complete editions of an author's works in a single literary form, use an appropriate collective title, also do the same for collections of three or more of his works limited to that form.

The most commonly used generic collective titles are:

1. "Correspondence" -- Used for collections of letters.

Twain, Mark, 1835-1910
   [Correspondence]
    Mark Twain's letters from Hawaii; edited and with an introduction by A. Grove Day. London, Chatto & Windus, 1967.

      xix, 298 p. 22½ cm. 30/–

                    (B 67–11305)

    I. Day, Arthur Grove, 1904–   ed. II. Title: Letters from Hawaii.

PS1331.A3 1967a   67–90409

Library of Congress   ₍3₎

Card 278

2. "Essays" -- This title is used for collections
of essays, short tracts, etc.

```
Emerson, Ralph Waldo, 1803-1882.
   [Essays]
   Five essays on man and nature; edited
by Robert E. Spiller.  New York, Appleton-
Century-Crofts [1954]
   viii, 120p.  18cm.
```

Card
279

3. "Novels" -- This will be used only for collections of novels and novelettes of
authors whose literary output is
principally novels and short stories;
in other cases "Prose works" would
be adequate.

```
Hemingway, Ernest, 1899-1961.
   [Novels]
   Three novels: The sun also rises; with an
introduction by Malcolm Cowley.  A farewell
to arms; with an introduction by Robert Penn
Warren.  The old man and the sea; with an
introduction by Carlos Baker.  New York,
Scribner [1962]
   xxviii, 247, xl, 332, xvii, 72p.  22cm.
```

Card
280

4. "Plays" -- To be used for collections of all
types of dramatic presentations such
as melodrama, comedy, tragedy, farce,
drama, etc.

Chekhov, Anton Pavlovich, 1860–1904.
   [Plays]
   Four plays. Translated and with a pref., afterwords,
and notes by Alex Szogyi. New York, Washington Square
Press ₁1968₁

   x. 288 p. 18 cm. $0.60

   CONTENTS.—The sea gull.—Uncle Vanya.—The three sisters.—
The cherry orchard.

   I. Szogyi, Alex, tr. II. Title.

PG3456.A13S9   72–166

Library of Congress   69 ₍3₎

Card
281

---

5. "Poems" -- In most cases this term will be
sufficient to cover all types of
poetry and verse, but there are cases
where it might seem more appropriate
to use a collective title for a particular style or type of poetry, e.g.
"Sonnets".

Poe, Edgar Allan, 1809-1849.
  [Poems]
  The complete poems of Edgar Allan Poe.
Prepared and edited with a commentary by
Louis Untermeyer. Illustrated with litho-
graphs by Hugo Steiner-Prag. New York,
Heritage Press [c1943]
    xxi, 214p. illus. 26cm.

Card
282

6. "Prose works" -- This is to be used for collections which consist of various types of prose writings, e.g. essays, novels, short stories, correspondence, criticism, etc.

Hawthorne, Nathaniel, 1804–1864.

  [Prose works]

    The scarlet letter, and other writings. Edited by H. Bruce Franklin. Philadelphia, Lippincott ₁1967₁

      vi, 310 p. 21 cm. (Contrasts in literature series)

      The Lippincott college English series.
      Preceptor, P. 22.

      CONTENTS.—The Custom-House.—The scarlet letter.—Main-street.—Ethan Brand.—Hawthorne's published critical writings.

      I. Franklin, Howard Bruce, ed. II. Title.

  PZ3.H318Sc 105   67–15511

  Library of Congress   ₁5₁

Card
283

---

7. "Short stories" -- Like the title "Novels" this one will be used for those authors whose literary production is mainly short stories and novels, otherwise "Prose works" could be used.

Maupassant, Guy de, 1850–1893.

  [Short stories]

    The diamond necklace, and four other stories. Illustrated by Robert Quackenbush. New York, F. Watts ₁1967₁

      82 p. illus. 23 cm.

      CONTENTS.—The diamond necklace.—The piece of string.—The Horla.—Two little soldiers.—The white wolf.

      I. Quackenbush, Robert M., illus. II. Title.

  PZ3.M445Di   67–17658

  Library of Congress   ₁3₁

Card
284

8. "Speeches" -- This uniform title can be used for collections of talks, addresses, lectures, speeches, orations, etc.

```
Roosevelt, Theodore, 1858-1919.
  [Speeches]
  Americanism and preparedness; speeches
July to November, 1916.  New York, Mail and
Express Job Print, 1917.
  145p.  23cm.
```
                                                    Card
                                                    285

The literary production of every author is unique in various ways and the categories just mentioned will be appropriate and sufficient for the works of most authors. The cataloger must establish the collective titles which best fit the works of any one author. In addition to the collective titles already discussed there are many others which could be established in special cases, e.g. "Anecdotes", "Fables", "Fairy tales", "Prayers", "Sermons", etc.

A generic collective title should not be assigned to a collection of writings to which the author himself assigned a title.

```
Henry, O., 1862-1910.
  Cabbages and kings.  New York, McClure,
Phillips & co., 1904.
  344p.  20cm.
```
                                                    Card
                                                    286

But, a collection of an author's works with a title chosen
by the editor or compiler should have a collective uniform
title so that similar collections of that author's works
will be grouped together.

Henry, O., 1862-1910.
    [Selected works]
    O. Henry's cops and robbers; O. Henry's
best detective and crime stories. Selected,
and with introduction by Ellery Queen.
New York, L. E. Spivak [c1948]
    123p. 20cm.

Card
287

107-E.   When a publication entered under any collective
         title is a translation (or in a foreign language if
         the alternative to rule 105 is followed), the lan-
         guage should be indicated in the same wa, as for
         an individual work, cf. rule 105.

Poe, Edgar Allan, 1809-1849.
    [Poems. Spanish]
    Los poemas de Edgar Poe. Traducción,
prólogo y notas por Carlos Obligado.
Buenos Aires, Espasa-Calpe [1942]
    171p. 21cm.

Card
288

Maupassant, Guy de, 1850-1893.
    [Short stories. French]
    Contes choisis. Edition pour la
jeunesse. Préface par Marcel Prevost.
Paris, Ollendorf, 1905.
    xii, 374p. 19cm.

Card
289

Shakespeare, William, 1564–1616.
[Works. German]
Werke. ([Nach der] Übersetzung von August Wilhelm von Schlegel [und] Dorothea und Ludwig Tieck mit den englischen Originalen verglichen und revidiert von Peter Plett) Hamburg, Hoffmann u. Campe (1966)
5 v. 19 cm. (Campe Klassiker) DM 70.–
(GDB 67-A12–238)
Nachwort von Wolfgang Clemen.

Card 290

Chekhov, Anton Pavlovich, 1860–1904.
[Plays. French]
Théâtre ... [par] Anton Tchékhov. Traduit et commenté par Elsa Triolet. Paris, Éditeurs français réunis, 1966.
2 v. (797 p.) 17 cm. (E. F. R. de poche) 6 F. each vol.
(F 66-5706)
Illustrated covers.

CONTENTS. — t. 1. Platonov. Ivanov. La mouette. — t. 2. L'oncle Vania. Les trois sœurs. La cerisaie. Le chant du cygne. L'ours. La demande en mariage. Le tragédien malgré lui. La noce. Le jubilé. Les méfaits du tabac.

I. Triolet, Elsa, tr.

PG3457.F5A19   1966

67–89787

Library of Congress   [2]

Card 291

107-F. When two works of an author are published together, use the uniform title of the first work and make an author-title added entry using the uniform title of the second work.

Chekhov, Anton Pavlovich, 1860-1904.
[The cherry orchard]
Two plays: The cherry orchard [and] Three sisters. With an introduction by John Gielgud and illustrations by Lajos Szalay. New York, Heritage Press, 1966.
xvi, 152p. illus.

I. Chekhov, Anton Pavlovich, 1860-1904. Three sisters. II. Title: Three sisters. III. Title: The cherry orchard.

Card 292

Chekhov, Anton Pavlovich, 1860-1904.
    Three sisters.
Chekhov, Anton Pavlovich, 1860-1904.
    [The cherry orchard]
    Two plays: The cherry orchard [and]
Three sisters. With an introduction by
John Gielgud and illustrations by Lajos
Szalay. New York, Heritage Press, 1966.
    xvi, 152p. illus.

Card
293

The cherry orchard.
Chekhov, Anton Pavlovich, 1860-1904.
    [The cherry orchard]
    Two plays: The cherry orchard [and]
Three sisters. With an introduction by
John Gielgud and illustrations by Lajos
Szalay. New York, Heritage Press, 1966.
    xvi. 152p. illus.

Card
294

Three sisters.
Chekhov, Anton Pavlovich, 1860-1904.
    [The cherry orchard]
    Two plays: The cherry orchard [and]
Three sisters. With an introduction by
John Gielgud and illustrations by Lajos
Szalay. New York, Heritage Press, 1966.
    xvi, 152p. illus.

Card
295

If the first title is not preceded by a collective title and it is the one which would be used for the work if published separately, then it is not necessary to interpose a uniform title.

```
Keyes, Frances Parkinson
   Lady Blanche Farm, and Queen
Anne's lace; two full length novels.
New York, Liveright /c1952/
   445p.  21cm.
                                              Card
                                              296
```

But, if there are three works in the publication a general collective title should be interposed according to the provisions of rule 107-E.

```
Albee, Edward
   /Plays/
   The zoo story, The death of Bessie
Smith /and/ The sandbox; three plays
introduced by the author.  New York,
Coward-McCann /c1960/
   158p.
                                              Card
                                              297
```

LIBRARY OF CONGRESS PRINTED CATALOG CARDS

Even though the Library of Congress is not currently making very extensive use of uniform titles, the following cards illustrate the use of interposed uniform titles in LC cataloging.

U. S. *Laws, statutes, etc.*
  ₍Social security act₎
  Law and Regulations. ₍Washington₎ Social Security
Administration, 1967–

  1 v. (loose-leaf) 27 cm.

  Contains Regulations promulgated by the Social Security Administration.

Card 298

Florida. *Laws, statutes, etc.*
  ₍Uniform commercial code₎
  The uniform commercial code of the State of Florida. Chapters 671–680, Florida statutes. ₍Tallahassee₎ Distributed by Tom Adams, secretary of state of the State of Florida in cooperation with Statutory Revision Dept., Attorney General's Office, 1965.

  101 p. 26 cm.

Card 299

Besard, Jean-Baptiste, *b. ca.* 1567.
  ₍Works. lute₎

  Oeuvres pour luth seul. Édition et transcription par André Souris. Étude biographique et appareil critique par Monique Rollin. Paris, Éditions du Centre national de la recherche scientifique, 1969.

  xiii, 165 p. 31 cm. (Collection Le Choeur des muses. Corpus des luthistes français)

Card 300

Boccherini, Luigi, 1743–1805.
  ₍Quintet, violins, viola, violoncellos, no. 83, D major. Grave; arr.₎

  Introduction and fandango. Arr. for guitar and harpsichord by Julian Bream. London, Faber Music; New York, G. Schirmer ₍1969₎

  score (12 p.) and part. 29 cm. ₍(Faber guitar series)

  1. Guitar and harpsichord music, Arranged. I. Bream, Julian, arr. II. Title.

  M277.B   73–222252

  Library of Congress   69 ₍1¾₎   M

Card 301

CHAPTER IV

SACRED SCRIPTURES -- Rules 108-118

Sacred scriptures are given special treatment in this section even though all are essentially the same as any other classical literary work for which the uniform title has been used as the main entry. The terms by which the sacred scriptures are known in English have been selected as the uniform titles, cf. rule 102-C-2.

Special rules for the sacred scriptures are necessary due to the vast quantity and variety of both complete and partial editions of these writings. The Bible is given special attention with very detailed rules which is understandable in view of the fact that the code was written for countries in which the Bible is the predominant sacred writing.

BIBLE.

108. <u>General rule.</u>

The uniform title "Bible" is used for the Bible and any of its parts except as noted in rule 109-E-1. The word "Bible" should be followed by these elements: (1) the designation of a part, cf. rule 109; (2) language of the text, cf. rule 110; (3) name of the version, translator or reviser, cf. rule 110; (4) year of imprint, cf. rule 113.

The AA rules have made a very logical improvement over the ALA rules by placing the version before the date in the heading, thus grouping the catalog cards by version rather than by date. Another major change is the entry of paraphrases on the Bible which are now entered under the paraphraser, cf. rule 7-A.

Bible. *English. Authorized. 1901.*
    The Holy Bible containing the Old and New Testaments: translated out of the original tongues: and with the former translations diligently compared and revised, by His Majesty's special command. Appointed to be read in churches. Glasgow, D. Bryce [1901]

Card
302

    1 v. (various pagings) facsim., plate. 49 mm.

    On cover: Illustrated miniature Bible.

    I. Title. II. Title: Illustrated miniature Bible.

BS185 1901.G55   65–59534

Library of Congress   [2]

---

109. Parts of the Bible.

109-A. Testaments and books. If the publication is one of
the Testaments the heading is composed thusly: (1) Bible,
(2) O.T. or N.T. as the case requires, (3) language of the
text, (4) version, (5) year of publication.

Bible. *N. T. English. Craddock. 1967.*
    The Christ Emphasis New Testament of Our Lord and
Saviour Jesus Christ. Translated out of the original tongues
and with the former translations diligently compared and
rev., King James version, 1611. By Edward J. Craddock.
Nashville, Bible Emphasis Publishers ₁1967₁

    532 p. 21 cm.

Card
303

    ɪ. Bible. N. T. English. Authorized. 1967. ɪɪ. Title.

BS2085 1967.N3   225.5'2'03   67–16877

Library of Congress   ₁5₁

    For a particular book of the Bible the heading is
arranged: (1) Bible, (2) O.T. or N.T. as needed, (3) name
of the book, (4) language of the text, (5) version, (6) year
of publication.

Bible. O.T. 2 Kings. Choctaw. Wright. 1871.
    The second book of Kings, translated into
the Choctaw language. Miko vhleha isht anumpa
atukla kvt toshowvt Chahta anumpa toba hoke.
New York, American Bible Society, 1871.
    p. [257] -339 18cm.

Card
304

Bible. *N. T. John. English. Authorized. 1967.*
    The Gospel according to Saint John, in the words of the
King James version of the year 1611. Edited in conformity
with the true ecumenical spirit of His Holiness, Pope John
xxɪɪɪ, by Dagobert D. Runes. New York, Philosophical
Library ₁1967₁

    vi. 97 p. 22 cm.

Card
305

    ɪ. Runes, Dagobert David, 1902-   ed. ɪɪ. Title.

BS2613. 1967   226'.5'05203   67–20465

Library of Congress   ₁3₁

Follow the same procedure for parts of books, but add to the name of the book the part or parts included in the publication being cataloged. Use as a guide the Authorized version for the numbering of books, chapters and verses. Use Arabic numerals for books and verses and Roman numerals for chapters.

Bible. O.T. Judges XIII, 2-7, 24-25 - XVI.
      English. Authorized. 1925.
Samson and Delilah from the book of Judges according to the authorised version. Waltham Saint Lawrence, Berkshire, Golden Cockerel Press, 1925.
    17p. illus. 27cm.

Card 306

Bible. N.T. Matthew IV, 23 - VIII, 1.
      English. Authorized. 1955.
The sermon on the Mount. Introduction by Norman Vincent Peale. Wood engravings by John De Pol. Cleveland, World Pub. Co. [1955]
    50p. illus. 21cm.

Card 307

Bible. N.T. John III, 16. Polyglot. 1872.
    St. John III, 16 in some of the langauges and dialects in which the Britsh & Foreign Bible Society has printed or circulated the Holy Scriptures. London, The British and Foreign Bible Society, 1872.
    30p. 19cm.

Card 308

109-B. Groups of books. For groups of books of the Bible which are commonly identified by a collective name the heading consists of: (1) Bible, (2) O.T. or N.T. as the case may be, (3) collective name, (4) language of the text, (5) version, (6) year of publication.

Bible. N.T. Gospels. English. Rieu. 1953.
    The four Gospels, a new translation from the Greek by E. V. Rieu. Baltimore, Penguin Books [1953]
      xxxiii, 250p. 19cm.

Card
309

109-C. Apocrypha. The books that comprise the Apocrypha are to be entered under: Bible. O.T. Apocrypha. Cf. rule 114.

Bible. O.T. Apocrypha. 1 Maccabees.
    English. Tedesche. 1962.
    The book of Maccabees. Translated by Sidney Tedesche. Illustrated by Jacob Shacham. Hartford, Prayer Book Press, 1962.
      78p. illus. 27cm.

Card
310

Bible. O.T. Apocrypha. English. Revised
    standard. 1957.
    The Apocrypha, Revised standard version of the Old Testament. Translated from the Greek and the Latin tongues being the version set forth A.D. 1611, rev. A.D. 1894, compared with the most ancient authorities and rev. A.D. 1957.
      250p. 22cm.

Card
311

109-D. References. Appropriate references should be made
under titles of individual books, their variant forms, the
collective names of groups of books, and wherever else references would be useful.

109-E. Selections.

109-E-1. Single selections. Enter a passage which is
better known by its title directly under the title and make
the appropriate reference from its citation as a part of
the Bible, cf. rule 102-C-2.

Lord's prayer.
 The Lord's prayer. ₁Munich, Waldmann & Pfitzner, ca. 1950₁

  2 l. 6 mm.

                 Card
                 312

Ten commandments. Polyglot.
 The Ten commandments, Exodus XX, 1-17, in
ancient and modern tongues. Compiled by
T. B. Khungian and A. B. Selian. Chicago,
Chicago Theological Seminary, 1893.
  54p. 20cm.

                 Card
                 313

109-E-2. Two selections. The same principle is applied
here as was used in rule 106-B-2 for two works. If two or
more selections or parts can be precisely encompassed by
two discreet headings for specific passages, books, or
groups of books with collective names, enter the publication under the heading for the first named on the title
page or the one that appears first in the publication and
make an added entry under the heading for the other part.

Bible. N.T. Gospels. English. Authorized. 1959.
    The Gospels of Saint Matthew, Saint Mark,
Saint Luke, & Saint John, together with the
Acts of the apostles, according to the
Authorized King James version, with reproductions
of religious paintings in the Samuel H. Kress
collection. New York, Arranged & printed by
R. Ellis for the Samuel H. Kress Foundation,
1959.
    253p. col. illus. 33cm.

Card
314

Bible. N.T. English. Moffatt. 1950.
    The New Testament and the Psalms; a new
translation by James Moffatt. New York,
Harper [c1950]
    561p. 11cm.

Card
315

I. Bible. O.T. Psalms. English. Moffatt.
    1950. II. Moffatt, James, 1870-1944, tr.

109-E-3. Other selections. For other selections and combi-
nations of three or more books that cannot be encompassed
by one or two of the group names listed in 109-B, miscellaneous excerpts, etc. the heading is under the most specific
Bible heading with the subheading "Selections" inserted just
before the year of publication. This follows the same
principle introduced in rule 106-B-3.

    If the selections were newly translated, however,
do not include the translator's surname in the heading as
indicated in 111-B.

Bible. O.T. English. Knox. Selections. 1960.
    Waiting for Christ, based on the translation
of the Old Testament messianic prophecies by
Ronald Knox, arranged in a continuous narrative
with explanations by Ronald Cox. New York,
Sheed & Ward [1960]
    282p. map. 22cm.

Card
316

Bible. O.T. Psalms. English. Douai.
      Selections. 1956.
    The child's book of Psalms. Selected by
Edith Lowe. Illustrated by Nan Pollard.
Garden City, N.Y., Garden City Books [1956]
    unpaged. illus. 29 x 14cm.

Card
317

Bible. English. Authorized. Selections. 1959.
    The prayers of the Bible. Compiled by
Philip Watters. Grand Rapids, Baker Book
House, 1959.
    334p. 23cm.

Card
318

Bible. *English. Revised standard Selections. 1967.*
    Bible readings in times of sorrow, selected by Bernice C.
Rich. London, T. Nelson [1967]

    60 p. 16 cm.

Card
319

    1. Consolation. I. Rich, Bernice C., comp. II. Title.

BV4901.R5   242.4   67–18849

Library of Congress   [3]

110. Language.

The name of the language is added after the word "Bible" if it is the whole Bible, or in the case of a part of the Bible the name of the language is added after the element that indicates the part or parts being cataloged.

However, if it has been decided that the library's policy is to follow the alternative rules to 101-A, 102-A and 105-A, then no language should be added to the heading when the text is in English. Only add the name of the language when it is not in English. This same principle should then be applied to rules 115-118 which cover other sacred scriptures.

Bible. *Authorized.* *1958.*
    The Holy Bible, containing the Old and New Testaments, translated out of the original tongues, and with the former translations diligently compared. Commonly known as the Authorized (King James) version. **Philadelphia, National Bible Press** ₁°1958₁
      1108, 64, 32 p. illus. (part col.) 8 col. maps. 21 cm.

Card 320

Bible. *Darby.* *1966.*
    The Holy Scriptures: a new translation from the original languages ₁by J. N. Darby.₁ ₁1st ed. reprinted₁ Kingston-on-Thames, Stow Hill Bible and Tract Depot, 1966.
      xxxii, 1510 p. 14 cm. 35/-   B***

Card 321

Bible. *N. T.* *Barclay.* *1968.*
    The New Testament: a new translation by William Barclay. London, New York, Collins, 1968-
      v. 24 cm. 25/- ($4.95) (v. 1)₁   B 68-23949

Card 322

Upanishads.
    The thirteen principal Upanishads. Translated from the Sanskrit with an outline of the philosophy of the Upanishads and an annotated bibliography by Robert Ernest Hume. With a list of recurrent and parallel passages by George C. O. Haas. 2d ed., rev. ₁Madras₁ Oxford University Press ₁1965₁
      xvi, 587 p. 23 cm. **Rs 15**
      Bibliography: p. 459-515.
      "Sixth impression"
      1. Philosophy, Hindu. 2. Upanishads—Bibl. I. Hume, Robert Ernest, 1877-1948, tr. II. Haas, George Christian Otto, 1883- ed. III. Title.

BL1120.A3H8 1965   S A 67-1740

                       PL 480: I-E-7343

Library of Congress   ₁3½₁

Card 323

111. <u>Version</u>.

The position of the name of the version in the heading now follows the name of the language. Previously this was the last element and it caused an awkward arrangement in the catalog by grouping editions of different versions by date of publication rather than arranging the various editions of the same version together.

The King James version, also known as the Authorized version, is always indicated in the heading by the word "Authorized".

Bible. *O. T. Psalms. English. Authorized. 1967.*
    The book of Psalms. Authorized or King James version from the Holy Bible. ₁Magnatype ed.₁ Pittsburgh, Stanwix House ₁1967₁

    417 p.   29 cm.

Card
324

ı. Title.

BS1422   1967   223′.2′05203   66–26066

Library of Congress   ₁5₁

1112.   <u>Alternative to version</u>.

At times it is necessary to substitute another term for the name of the version. Substitutions are made in the following cases which are listed in order of preference: (1) when the text is in the original language, (2) when the version is unknown, (3) if the version has been altered, (4) if the version cannot be identified by a name or by its translator's name, or (5) when more than two versions are involved.

Substitutions which can be made for versions are: (a) the name of the manuscript or its repository designation when the work is a manuscript or a reproduction, transcription, edition, or translation thereof, (b) the surname of a person who has altered the text when an altered text has no name of its own, (c) any special name or phrase that is used on the title page to identify the particular edition.

If no useful identification can be made, this element may be omitted from the heading.

113. <u>Year</u>.

The year of imprint is always the last element included in the heading.

When the name of a manuscript or a repository designation is used as an alternative to the version the date can be omitted.

114. <u>Apocryphal books</u>.

The term "apocrypha" and its adjectival form "apocryphal" mean secret or not canonical and are commonly used to refer to religious writings of dubious authenticity. There are many books which are considered as "apocryphal" by Jews, Protestants, and Roman Catholics, e.g. Book of jubilees, Assumption of Moses, Ascension of Isiah, Odes of Solomon, Apocalypse of Abraham, Apocalypse of Baruch. Each apocryphal book is entered under its title the same as any anonymous classic is entered under a uniform title, cf. rule 102-C-2.

There are also certain apocryphal books which are accepted as canonical by some religions and are appended to the Old Testament. There is one certain group of these books which is considered by some to be canonical; it is known as the "Apocrypha" and includes only those books listed in rule 109-C, and are entered according to that rule. Any apocryphal book excluded from that list is to be treated as not canonical and the provisions of rule 114 are applied. Collections of apocryphal books are entered according to the provisions of rule 5.

```
Book of jubilees.
    The Book of jubilees. Translated from the
Ethiopic by Rev. George H. Schodde. Oberlin, O.,
E.J. Goodrich, 1888.
    xv, 131p. 23cm.
                                              Card
                                              325
```

James, Montague Rhodes, 1862-1966
   Apocrypha anecdota, a collection of thirteen
apocryphal books and fragments now first edited
from manuscripts by Montague Rhodes James.
Cambridge, The University Press, 1893.
      x, 202p. 22cm.

Card
326

Rules 115-118 indicate the uniform titles which are
to be used with sacred writings of certain non-Christian
religions. Included are names of parts of some of these
writings with examples to illustrate the proper form of
entries. Basically all of these scriptures are treated the
same as the Bible and its parts. Generally, there is not
as much detail used in the headings for these other sacred
writings, due to the fact that most North American libraries
will not have very large collections of these works.

115. Jewish scriptures other than the Bible.

There are two headings commonly used for the Talmud.
The uniform title for the Babylonian Talmud is "Talmud",
and for the Palestinian or Jerusalem Talmud "Talmud Yerushalmi"
is used as the uniform title.

Talmud. English.
   The Babylonian Talmud. Translated into
English with notes, glossary, and indices
under the editorship of I. Epstein. London,
Soncino Press, 1935-48.
      34v. 24cm.

Card
327

Talmud Yerushalmi. English. Selections.
The Talmud of Jerusalem. With a preface
by Dagobert D. Runes. New York, Wisdom
Library [1956]
160p. 19cm.

Card
328

116. Buddhist scriptures.

Collections of Buddhist scriptures are entered under
the uniform title "Tripitaka". Component divisions of the
Tripitaka and their component treatises are entered directly
under their own titles.

Tripitaka. English. Selections.
Early Buddhist scriptures; a selection,
translated and edited by Edward J. Thomas.
London, K. Paul, Trench, Trubner & Co., 1935.
xxv, 232p. 23cm.

Card
329

Jatakas. *German. Selections.*
Buddhistische Märchen aus dem alten Indien. (Aus-
gewählt und übertragen von Else Lüders. Nachwort von
Heinrich Lüders) (Düsseldorf, Köln) Diederichs [1965]
406 p. 20 cm. (Die Märchen der Weltliteratur) DM 16.80

(GDB 66–A43–106)

Card
330

1. Folk-lore—India.   I. Lüders, Else   Peipers   1880–
II. Title.   (Series)

GR305.J3   1965   67–83954

Library of Congress   [2]

117. Hindu, Jain, Sikh, and Zoroastrian scriptures.

The most commonly known religious writings of Hinduism are the Vedic texts, the Aranyakas, Brahmanas, Upanishads and the sutras. For the Vedic texts use the uniform title, "Vedas". See Fig. Use "Aranyakas", "Brahmanas", and "Upanishads" for collections of these texts, and for an anonymous sutra use the title as its uniform heading.

Vedas. Rigveda. English. Selections.
  Hymns to the Mystic Fire; hymns to Agni
from the Rig Veda, translated in their
esoteric sense [by] Sri Aurobindo. [Pondicherry,
Sri Aurobindo Ashram, 1946]
  xlviii, 191p. 23cm.

Card
331

Upanishads. *English.*
  The thirteen principal Upanishads. Translated from the Sanskrit with an outline of the philosophy of the Upanishads and an annotated bibliography by Robert Ernest Hume. With a list of recurrent and parallel passages by George C. O. Haas. 2d ed., rev. [Madras] Oxford University Press [1965]
    xvi, 587 p. 23 cm. **Rs 15**
    Bibliography: p. 459–515.
    "Sixth impression"
    1. Philosophy, Hindu. 2. Upanishads—Bibl. I. Hume, Robert Ernest, 1877–1948, tr. II. Haas, George Christian Otto, 1883–   ed. III. Title.

  BL1120.A3H8   1965   S A 67–1740

                                          PL 480: I–E–7343

  Library of Congress   [3½]

Card
332

Use the uniform title "Siddhanta" for collections of the sacred texts of Jainism.

For the sacred scriptures of the Sikhs use the uniform title "Adi-Granth".

The various texts of the Zoroastrian canon known collectively as the "Avesta" are entered under this as a uniform title.

118. Islamic scriptures.

Use "Koran" as the uniform title for the Koran and
its parts.

Koran. *English. Selections.*
  Wisdom of the Koran. Edited by C. Merton Babcock,
and illustrated with wood-engravings by Boyd Hanna.
Mount Vernon, N. Y.. Peter Pauper Press ₁1966₁

  62 p. illus. 19 cm.

Card
333

  ɪ. Babcock, Clarence Merton, ed. ɪɪ. Hanna, Boyd, illus. ɪɪɪ. Peter
Pauper Press, Mount Vernon, N. Y. ɪᴠ. Title.

BP110.B3   297'.122   67–1430

Library of Congress   ₁3₁

Koran. *French.*
  Le Coran ... Préface par J. Grosjean. Introduction,
traduction et notes par D. Masson. ₁Paris,₁ Gallimard, 1967.
  cxvi, 1088 p. maps. 18 cm. (Bibliothèque de la Pléiade, v. 190)
45 F.

                                        (F 67–4543)
  Bibliography: p. ₁1013₁–1016.

Card
334

  ɪ. Masson, Denise, ed.

BP112.M3   297'.1225'4   67–98998

Library of Congress   ₁2₁

CONFERENCES, CONGRESSES, MEETINGS, ETC. AND RADIO AND TELEVISION STATIONS. Rules 87-91 and 97.

Conferences, congresses, meetings, etc.

The rules 87-91 are to be applied to all types of conferences, institutes, symposia, meetings, workshops, etc. The whole approach of the AA rules is quite different from that of the ALA rules in that the new code treats all conferences, congresses, meetings, etc. in the same way, whereas the ALA rules attempted to categorize each type of meeting and treat it differently. In many cases the heading is the same whether done by the AA or the ALA rules. Of important significance is the fact that the AA rules do not require the vast number of references as did the ALA rules.

Rules 87-91 apply only to groups of persons, either as individuals or as representatives of various bodies, who have come together to study, discuss or act on a particular topic or on various topics of common interest.

Conference on Developments in Geography, *Moray House College of Education, 1964.*
    Developments in geography; papers from a conference for secondary school teachers, 3rd and 4th July, 1964. Edinburgh, Moray House College of Education, 1965.

    ix, 97 p. map, tables, diagr. 22 cm. (Moray House publications, no. 3) 4/–

(B 67-2189)

Card 335

National Conference on X-Ray Technician Training. *College Park, Md., 1966.*
    National Conference on X-Ray Technician Training: [proceedings] Rockville, Md., U. S. Dept. of Health, Education, and Welfare, Public Health Service, Training Branch, Division of Radiological Health [1966]

    v. 84 p. 26 cm.

    1. Radiology—Study and teaching—Congresses.   I. U. S. Public Health Service. Division of Radiological Health.

RMS49.N3 1966   616.07'572   67–60205

Library of Congress   [8]

Card 336

A group of members of an organization who convene as representatives of that organization or a subdivision thereof is treated under the provisions of rules 69 and 70.

American Association of Petroleum Geologists.
　　Diapirism and diapirs; a symposium, including papers presented at the 50th annual meeting of the Association in New Orleans, Louisiana, April 26-29, 1965, and some others. Edited by Jules Braunstein and Gerald D. O'Brien. Tulsa, Okla., 1968.

　　　vii, 444 p. illus., maps. 25 cm. (*Its* Memoir 8)

　　　Bibliography: p. 358-414.

　　　1. Diapirs—Congresses. 2. Diapirs—Bibl. ɪ. Braunstein, Jules, ed. ɪɪ. O'Brien, Gerald D., ed. ɪɪɪ. Title. (Series)

QE606.A48　　　　　　　551.8　　　　　　　68-16891

Library of Congress　　　　ₗ7ₗ　　　　　　BOS

Card
337

87.　General rule.

　　A conference, congress or other meeting is to be entered under its name, and generally followed by one or more of the following elements:　number, place and date.

State House Conference on Education. *2d, Columbus, Ohio,* *1961.*
　　The people speak; a summary report, by William Fulwider.　Columbus ₗ1961ₗ

　　　57 p. 23 cm.

Card
338

International Conference of Printing Research Institutes, *8th, Aulanko, 1965.*
　　Paper in the printing processes; proceedings.　Edited by W. H. Banks.　Oxford, New York, Symposium Publications Division, Pergamon Press ₗ1967ₗ
　　　viii, 454 p. illus. 23 cm. (Advances in printing science and technology, v. 4)
　　　"Conference ... met ... under its new organization, the International Association of Research Institutes for the Graphic Arts Industry."
　　　Includes bibliographies.
　　　1. Paper—Printing properties—Congresses. ɪ. Banks, William H., ed. ɪɪ. International Association of Research Institutes for the Graphic Arts Industry. ɪɪɪ. Title. (Series)

Z247.I 52　1965　　　　　655.3　　　　　　67-13995

Library of Congress　　　　ₗ7ₗ

Card
339

Care must be taken to assure that the meeting or conference is considered to have a name of its own and not just a general description. The footnote to rule 87 explains in detail hów to determine whether or not a conference or meeting has a specific apellation. For examples of meetings lacking a specific name see the following cards.

The **Impact** of the Public Law 480 program on overseas acquisitions by American libraries; proceedings of a conference. Edited by William L. Williamson. ₍Madison₎ Library School, University of Wisconsin, 1967.

II, 41 l. 28 cm.

Card 340

New rules for an old game; proceedings of a workshop on the 1967 Anglo-American cataloguing code held by the School of Librarianship, The University of British Columbia, April 13 and 14, 1967. Edited by Thelma E. Allen ₍and₎ Daryl Ann Dickman. Vancouver, Publications Centre, University of British Columbia, 1967.

Card 341

175 p. 24 cm. unpriced

(C***)

Bibliography: p. 161–₍165₎

1. Cataloging—Congresses. I. Allen, Thelma E., ed. II. Dickman, Daryl Ann, ed. III. British Columbia. University. School of Librarianship. IV. Title: Anglo-American cataloguing code.

Z695.N4892   025.3'2   67–29572

Library of Congress   ₍2₎

If a heading is required for a projected meeting that was never held, establish the heading as if it had been held, but add "(Projected, not held)" at the end of the heading.

International Congress of Anthropology and Prehistoric Archæology. *18th, Istanbul and Ankara, 1939 (Projected, not held)*
    XVIII inci ₍i. e. On sekizinci₎ Beynelmilel Antropoloji ve Prehistorik Arkeoloji Kongresi, İstanbul-Ankara, 18–25 Eylûl 1939. Ankara, 1939.

2 v. plates. 23 cm.

"Le XVIIIᵉ Congrès international d'anthropologie et d'archéologie préhistorique ... a dû être remis à une date indéterminée, par suite de la guerre européenne qui éclata au début de septembre 1939."—v. 2, p. ₍vii₎
    Contributions and translations in English, French, German, or Turkish.

Card 342

N E 61–85

88. Name.

   Enter a conference under its specific name even if
it has a more general name as one of a series of conferences.

   Omit words in the name of a conference that denote
its number, frequency, or year of convocation.

89. Number.

   If a conference is one of a series of numbered conferences of the same name follow the name by the abbreviation of the ordinal number in English, regardless of the
fact that the name of the conference may be in another language.

Symposium in Pure Mathematics. *4th, University of Cali-*
fornia, 1960.
   Partial differential equations. Proceedings of the fourth
Symposium in Pure Mathematics of the American Mathematical Society. Charles B. Morrey, Jr., editor. Providence, American Mathematical Society, 1961.
   vi, 169 p. 26 cm. (Proceedings of Symposia in Pure Mathematics,
v. 4)
   Includes bibliographies.

Card
343

Symposium in Pure Mathematics. *5th, New York, 1961.*
   Recursive function theory. ₍Proceedings of the Fifth
Symposium in Pure Mathematics of the American Mathematical Society₎ Providence, American Mathematical Society, 1962.

   vii, 247 p. illus., port. 26 cm. (Proceedings of Symposia in Pure
Mathematics, v. 5)
   Includes bibliographies.

Card
344

Congreso Internacional de Pireneístas. *3d, Gerona, Spain,*
1958.
   Actas. ₍Zaragoza₎ Instituto de Estudios Pirenaicos, Con-
sejo Superior de Investigaciones Científicas ₍1962–
        v.   illus., maps (part fold.) profiles. 25 cm.
   Spanish and French.
   Includes bibliographies.
   CONTENTS.—t. 1. Geología, morfología y geofísica.—t. 2. Clima-
tología, edafología, botánica y zoología.—

   t. 4. Geografía.—

   t. 6. Filología.
      1. Pyrenees.   I. Spain. Consejo Superior de Investigaciones
Científicas. Instituto de Estudios Pirenaicos.

   DC611.P981C63   1958ae   67–50725

   Library of Congress   ₍2₎

Card
345

90. Place.

90-A.   The name of the place where a conference was held follows the name or the number.

Meeting on Fish Technology, *Scheveningen, 1964.*
    Fish handling and preservation; proceedings. Paris, Organisation for Economic Co-operation and Development, 1965.

324 p. illus. 24 cm.

Card 346

Congress "Pro Aqua." *3d. Basel, 1965.*
    Wasser und Luft in der Raumplanung. Eau et air dans les plans d'aménagement. Water and air in land development. Bericht über die Internationale Vortragstagung Pro Aqua 1965 in Basel. (Hrsg. von der Pro Aqua A G Basel. Redaktion: Hansjörg Schmassmann) Mit 166 Abbildungen. München, Wien, Oldenbourg, 1966.

viii, 424 p. with maps (part fold.) 24 cm. DM 116.-

(GDR***)

German, French or English. Summaries in German, French and English.
Includes bibliographies.
1. Pollution—Congresses. 2. Water-supply—Congresses. 3. Sewage disposal—Congresses. I. Pro Aqua A. G., Basel. II. Title.

TD5.C69 1965c

67–86159

Library of Congress

Card 347

90-B.   If the name of the institution at which a conference was held provides a better identification, prefer this name to the geographic name of the place.

Seminar in Effective Labour Relations, *Assumption University of Windsor, 1960.*
    Effective labour relations; report of proceedings. (Windsor, Ont.) School of Business Administration, Essex College, Assumption University of Windsor (1960?)

Card 348

Summer Institute in Nuclear and Particle Physics, *McGill University, 1967.*
    Nuclear and particle physics. Editors: B. Margolis and C. S. Lam; associate editor: N. de Takacsy. Amsterdam, New York, W. A. Benjamin, 1968.

547 p. 24 cm. unpriced

(Ne***)

"Held ... under the auspices of the Theoretical Physics Division of the Canadian Association of Physicists"
Includes bibliographies.

1. Particles (Nuclear physics)—Addresses, essays, lectures. I. Margolis, Bernard, ed. II. Lam, Harry C. S., ed. III. Canadian Association of Physicists. Theoretical Physics Division. IV. Title.

QC721.S85 1967

539.7

68–25423

Library of Congress   (5)   BOS

Card 349

90-C.   If the sessions of one conference were held in two
places, use both names.

Reunión Internacional de Ejecutivos de la Reforma Agraria.
1st, Lima and Bogotá, 1965.
   Informe de la Reunión Internacional de Ejecutivos de la
Reforma Agraria, y de la Reunión de Evaluación y Pla-
neamiento del Proyecto 206. Lima-Bogotá, 1965. ₍1. ed.₎
Bogotá, IICA–CIRA, 1966.
   132 p. 28 cm.
   At head of title: Instituto Interamericano de Ciencias Agrícolas
de la OEA. Centro Interamericano de Reforma Agraria. Proyecto
206 del Programa de Cooperación Técnica de la Organización de
Estados Americanos.

Card
350

**International Congress of European and Western Ethnol-
ogy,** *Stockholm and Uppsala, 1951.*
   Papers. ₍Editor: Sigurd Erixon₎ Published under the
auspices of the International Council for Philosophy and
Humanistic Studies (CIPSH) and with the support of
UNESCO, by the International Commission on Folk Arts
and Folklore (CIAP) and the Swedish Organizing Committee of the congress. Stockholm, 1955.
   159 p. illus., group port. 22 cm.
   English, French, or German.
   Includes bibliographies.
   1. Ethnology—Congresses.   i. Erixon, Sigurd Emanuel, 1888–
ed.

GN3.I 53   1951ac   62–25511

Library of Congress

Card
351

If there are more than two places, use only the
principal one or the one named first followed by "etc.

Congreso de la Emigración Española a Ultramar, *2d, Coruña, etc., 1959.*
   ii ₍i. e. Segundo₎ Congreso de la Emigración Española a
Ultramar. ₍Madrid₎ Ministerio de Trabajo, Instituto Español de Emigración ₍1960₎
   225 p. illus. (part col.) 28 cm.
   "Convocado por el Círculo de Estudios Migratorios de La Coruña."
   CONTENTS.—Discursos y mensajes.—Conferencias.—Calendario.—
Conclusiones del Congreso. — Ponencias y Comunicaciones. — Docu-
mentos.
   1. Spain—Emig. & immig.—Congresses.   i. Círculo de Estudios
Migratorios de La Coruña.

JV8251.Z6   1959   67–46365

Library of Congress   ₍2₎

Card
352

91. <u>Date</u>.

As the last element in the heading add the year in which the conference was held if the heading is for s single conference. Specific dates are used if it is necessary to identify the meeting or distinguish it from another.

Conference on Children Born Out of Wedlock. *1st, Harrisburg, Pa., 1965*
    The report. ₁Harrisburg, 1965₁

    2 v. 28 cm.

Card 353

Institute on Marriage, the Family, and Human Sexuality, *Wake Forest College, 1966.*
    Marriage, the family, and human sexuality in medical education; report. ₁Winston-Salem, N. C., 1966₁

    39 p. 23 cm.

Card 354

Intergovernmental Conference on Copyright, *Geneva, 1952.*
    Universal copyright convention, an analysis and commentary, by Arpad Bogsch. New York, R. R. Bowker, 1958.

    xx, 279 p. 24 cm.

Card 355

International Colloquium on Luso-Brazilian Studies. *6th, Cambridge, Mass. and New York, 1966.*
    Europe informed; an exhibition of early books which acquainted Europe with the East. Cambridge, Massachusetts: Harvard College Library; New York, New York: New York Public Library, Columbia University Library, Library of the Hispanic Society of America. ₁Cambridge? 1966₁

    x, 192 p. illus., facsims. 23 cm.

Card 356

Western American Assembly on the Ombudsman, *Berkeley, Calif., 1968.*
    Report. Stanley Scott, editor. ₁Berkeley, Institute of Governmental Studies, University of California₁ 1968.

    vii, 36 p. 23 cm. $1.00

    Sponsored by the Institute of Governmental Studies, University of California, Berkeley; the Institute for Local Self Government, Berkeley; and the American Assembly, Columbia University.

    1. Ombudsman—U. S.   ɪ. Scott, Stanley, 1921– ed. ɪɪ. California. University. Institute of Governmental Studies. ɪɪɪ. Institute for Local Self Government. ɪᴠ. American Assembly. **Title**

    JK468.O6W47   353.009   68–65922

    Library of Congress   ₁3₁

Card 357

Radio and television stations.

97.   Radio and television stations.

This rule is numbered 98 in the British text, but the text and the examples are identical.

This is one of the few cases in the AA rules where main entries begin with letters rather than a word. If the call letters constitute the primary or sole identifying element of the name of a radio or television station, it is entered under its call letters followed by either " (Radio station) " or " (Television station) " and the place with which the station is identified. Even if a television station's call letters contain the letters "TV", the phrase " (Television station) " is added after the call letters,
      E.g. WMAQ-TV (Television station) Chicago

Radio and television stations whose main entries are not under call letters are entered according to the general rules 60-71, with the exception that if the name of the place with which the section is identified does not appear in its name, it is added at the end. This addition of a place name is an exception to rule 65.

WQXR (Radio station) New York
   Programs. no. 1-
New York, Interstate Broadcasting Co., 1939-
   no. in v. illus. 24cm. monthly.

Card 358

WGN (Radio station) Chicago
   WGN; a pictoral history. Based on a
company history by Francis Coughlin.
General supervision [by] Daniel Calibraro.
Text [by] John Fink. Design [by] Robert
Snyder and Associates. Chicago, 1961.
   191p. illus.

Card 359

CHAPTER VI

GENERAL RULES FOR CORPORATE BODIES -- Rules 60-71

For cataloging purposes a corporate body is considered to be any organization or group of persons that is
identified by a name and that acts or may act as an entity.
There are many kinds of organizations and groups which are
classed as corporate bodies, some of those that are most
frequently encountered are associations, business firms,
churches, conferences, expeditions, governments and their
specific agencies, institutions and non-profit enterprises.

The AA rules demonstrate great advances in cataloging by the simplification and improvement of headings for
corporate bodies. There is no doubt that the group of rules
for corporate bodies offers more to the simplification of
cataloging than any other part of the AA rules, not only by
making it simpler for the cataloger, but also easier for
the library user to locate material in the catalog. Catalogers should never lose sight of the fact that the catalog
is intended mainly for the library's clientele and not
solely for other librarians. A cataloging code that reduces
the efforts of the cataloger and at the same time improves
the catalog by making it an easier tool for everyone to use
is a real credit to those responsible for its contents.
The Anglo-American Cataloging Rules is just such a code; a
large part of its superiority over other cataloging codes
is due to the simplicity of the rules for corporate bodies.

This guide to the AA rules is intended for use with
the North American text, but it is felt that an explanation
of the North American text without comparing it to the
British text would be unjust. The advantages of the British
text are mainly due to the fact that it remained more faith-
ful to the "Statement of Principles" as adopted by the
International Conference on Cataloguing Principles in Paris
in 1961 and commonly referred to as the "Paris Principles".
American librarians should be well aware of the greater
simplicity and logic that permeate the British text and
they should know wherein exist the deviations that make the
North American text inferior to the British text.

The very basic concept of exactly what is a corporate body differs in the two texts. In the North American text the word, "churches" was dropped from the list of examples of types of corporate bodies which were included at the end of the definition.

60. Basic Rule.

The fundamental concept on which the rules to determine headings for corporate bodies are based is that each one is to be entered under its own name. There are exceptions included in the subsequent rules which provide for its entry under a higher body of which it is a part, under the name of the government of which it is an agency, or under the name of the place in which it is located.

The British text does not include the last phrase, "or under the name of the place in which it is located". This was added to the North American text to continue an old practice of entering certain types of corporate bodies under the name of the city in which they are located, regardless of the fact that they may or may not be known by the name of the place in which they are located, or whether they are better known by their own names.

EXAMPLES: Aerodromo de Puerto Juarez
Biblioteca Nacional do Rio de Janeiro
British Museum
Carnegie Library of Pittsburgh
City Library, Cohoes
Colin Buchanan and Partners
Ecole centrale lyonnaise
Memorial Hospital, Fort Lauderdale
Paddington Chamber of Commerce
Public Library of Cincinnati and Hamilton County
Radio Society of Great Britain
State Teachers College, Bridgewater
Universitat Heidelberg
Universite libre de Bruxelles
University of Kansas
University of Texas at El Paso
Yale University

61. General Rule.

The form of a corporate body's name as it is most commonly found in its own publications, albeit the author, publisher, or sponsor of its publications, should be preferred over a variant form of the name found in reference sources.

62. <u>Variant forms in the publications.</u>

      It is not uncommon that different forms of a name will appear in the publications of a corporate body. Parts A through D list in the order of preference criteria to consider to determine the best form to be used for the heading.

62-A.   Brief form. A brief form that provides adequate identification for cataloging purposes should be preferred.

62-A-1. Use a brief form which consists of the initial letters of the words or principal words of its name if it is written in capital and lower case letters.

62-A-2. Use a brief form which is made up of syllables of the words or of the principle words of its name, or of a combination of syllables and initial letters.

62-B.   Official form. If a variant form which is used in a body's publications does not provide adequate identification, the official form of the name should be preferred whenever found.

62-C.   Predominant form. The predominant form used in a body's publications should be used when a brief form is not available and the official form is not known.

62-D.   Most recent form. If no single predominant form can be determined, the form most recently used at the time of establishing the heading should be used.

63. <u>Conventional name.</u>

63-A.   A body which is more frequently identified by a conventional name in the reference sources in its own language, should be entered under this conventional form of the name rather than the official name and any other forms of name used in its publications.

63-B.   The form of the name chosen for bodies which are either international in character or of ancient origin should always be the English form if there is one that became firmly established in English language usage, regardless of the form that might appear on its publications. The most common types of bodies which fall into this category are religious bodies, fraternal and knightly orders, and diplomatic congresses.

64. Language.

       If the name of a corporate body appears in different
languages prefer the form in the official language, except
as qualified in 64-A. If there is more than one official
language, one of which is English, the English is preferred.
If English is not one of the official languages or if the
official language is not known, use the form in the language
predominantly used in the publications; in case of doubt,
prefer English, French, German, Spanish or Russian in this
order.

65. Additions to names.

       The reason for adding a word or phrase to the name
of a corporate body is that often two or more bodies have
the same name or names which are so similar that they are
likely to be confused. These bodies with similar names
are distinguished by adding a word or phrase to the name
of each unless one of them is so much better known by the
users of the catalog that it would be correctly understood
without the addition of a term.

       Too often this is incorrectly interpreted to mean
that a body with a rather undistinguished name such as
"Library Association" or "National Archives" needs to have
an addition to its name; if there is no other body with
that exact same name represented in the catalog, then a
term does not need to be added. Terms are only added when
the bodies with similar names are represented, or likely
to be represented, in the same catalog.

       Follow the order of preference indicated in Parts A
through D in selecting terms to distinguish between bodies
with the same name.

65-A. Local Place names.

       Add the name of the place in which the body is lo-
cated if the same name has been used by another body in a
different location.

65-A-1. Use the name of the specific local political jurisdiction, such as the name of the city, town or other local
jurisdiction below the county level or its equivalents.
Local place names and names of institutions used as distinguishing terms follow the name of the body and are separated
by a comma. The purpose here is to identify and distinguish
between corporate bodies with identical names, and not to
locate; hence the name of the state is not usually necessary.

St. John's University, *Collegeville*. *Library*.
Dedication: Saint John's University Library, Collegeville, Minnesota, 1966, May. ₁Collegeville, 1966₁

1 v. (unpaged) 31 cm.

Card
360

St. John's University, New York.
Saint Vincent de Paul, a tercentenary
commemoration of his death, 1660-1960.
Jamaica, N.Y., St. John's University
Press, 1960.
108p. illus. 26cm.

Card
361

65-B. Names of countries, states, provinces, etc.

The name of the country, state or province is added
in parentheses as the distinguishing term for those bodies
which have a character that is national, state, provincial,
etc., or which have a local place name as a part of the corporate name that is insufficient to differentiate two or
more bodies.

People's National Party (Jamaica)
Constitution of the People's National Party.
Kingston ₁City Printery, 19--₁
21 p. 21 cm.

Card
362

Democratic Labour Party (Barbados)
Democratic Labour Party, 1955-1965; ten
years of service. ₁Bridgetown₁ Advocate
Commercial Printing ₁1965 or 6₁
21 p. illus. 25 cm.
Cover title.

Card
363

65-C. Years of founding.

The year of founding or the inclusive years of existence are added as the distinguishing term for those bodies that cannot be distinguished by place.

65-D. Other additions.

If a place or date is insufficient or inappropriate to distinguish between bodies as suitable disignation or qualifying term is added in parentheses. When a name alone does not convey the idea of a corporate body an appropriate general qualifying term is added.

Laurence Witten (*Firm*)
Catalogue.
New Haven ¡Conn., 19

v. facsims. 28 cm.

Card
364

Steuben Glass (Firm)
Poetry in crystal; interpretations in crystal of thirty-one new poems by contemporary American poets. ¡1st ed. New York, 1963¡

86 p. illus. 28 cm.

Card
365

Louvre (Museum) **Département des antiquités grecques et romaines.**

La sculpture grecque et romaine au Musée du Louvre, par Jean Charbonneaux.   Paris, Ed. des Musées nationaux, 1963.
4 l., 289 ¡2¡ p. 208 illus., plan. 17 cm.
(Collection des guides du visiteur)

Card
366

Santa Maria del Carmine (Convent)
The library of the Carmelites at Florence at the end of the fourteenth century, by K. W. Humphreys. Amsterdam, Erasmus Booksellers, 1964.

104 p. 26 cm. (Studies in the history of libraries and librarianship, v. 2)

Safaho monographs, v. 3.
"400 copies printed."
Contains an "Inventory of the library," chiefly in Latin; with prefatory matter, "Index of authors" with their works, and an "Index of incipits," by K. W. Humphreys.

Card
367

66. Omissions from names.

66-A. Initial articles.

Always drop initial articles that are not needed for reasons of clarity or grammar.

66-B. Initial adjectives denoting royal privilege.

Initial adjectives that denote royal privilege should always be dropped from names in any European language except English, regardless of the fact that it may be either abbreviated or written in full. However, if the elimination of this adjective would reduce the name to a common word or phrase, then it should be retained; whenever in doubt, retain it.

Kongelige Bibliotek.
      Current Danish periodicals; a select list.
Copenhagen, The Royal library, 1965.
      45 p.
	Card
	368

Kungliga Biblioteket.
      Illuminated manuscripts and other remarkable documents from the collections of the Royal Library, Stockholm. Catalogue of an exhibition, June–September 1963. ₁Stockholm, 1963 ₁
      31 p. 16 plates (part col.) 21 cm.
	Card
	369

Royal Ontario Museum.
      Canadian textiles, 1750-1900, an exhibition
Toronto, 1965.
      1 v.
	Card
	370

Royal Institute of Public Administration. *Local Government Operational Research Unit.*
      Performance and size of local education authorities. London, H. M. S. O., 1968.
 	
      v, 183 p. illus., forms. 25 cm. (Royal Commission on Local Government in England. Research studies, 4) 15/-
 	
                    (B 68–10538)
 	
      1. School management and organization—England—Stat. 2. Educational statistics.   I. Title.   (Series: Gt. Brit. Local Government Commission for England. Research studies, 4)
 	
      JS3111.A38 no. 4   354′.0085   68–131978
 	
      Library of Congress   ₍2₎
	Card
	371

66-E. Terms ·indicating incorporation and certain other terms.

Adjectival terms and appositive nouns or phrases that designate a particular type of incorporation should be omitted if they are not regarded as integral parts of the corporate name and they are not needed to make clear that the name is that of a corporate body.

Continental Aviation & Engineering Corporation.
  Preliminary model specification, turbojet aircraft engine, continental model CJ69-1400.
  Detroit, 1960.
     67 l. illus. 28 cm.

Card 372

Little, Brown and Company.
  One hundred and twenty-five years of publishing, 1837–1962. [1st ed.] Boston [1962]
     84 p. illus. 20 cm.

Card 373

I. Title.

Z473.L7627   655.47446   62—1454 ‡
                                          FEB 5 63 AD

Library of Congress   [62f5]

67. Modification of names.

67-A. Initials and abbreviations of forenames.

When the corporate name begins with one or more abbreviations or initials of a forename followed by a surname, place them in parentheses after the surname in the heading.

Du Pont de Nemours (E. I.) and Company.
  Du Pont, the autobiography of an American enterprise; the story of E. I. du Pont de Nemours & Company, published in commemoration of the 150th anniversary of the founding of the company on July 19, 1802. Wilmington, Del.; distributed by Scribner, New York [1952]
     138 p. illus. 31 cm.

Card 374

I. Title.

HD9651.9.D8A5   662.2065   52–2583 rev

Library of Congress   [r65x‡]

Lippincott (J. B.) Company
    The author and his audience; with a chronology of major events in the publishing history of J. B. Lippincott Company. ₍Philadelphia, 1967₎

    79 p. 22 cm.

Card 375

Wells (H.G.) Society
    H. G. Wells: a comprehensive bibliography; compiled by the H. G. Wells Society, with a foreword by Kingsley Martin. 2nd ed. (revised). London, H. G. Wells Society, 1968.

    vi, 69 p. 19 cm. 30/-

Card 376

Agnew (Thos.) & Sons.
    Baroque and Rococo in Italy. Illustrated catalogue. ₍Exhibition₎ May 2 - May 27, 1966. ₍London, 1966₎

Card 377

Lochner (H.W.) and Company.
    Madison-St. Clair Counties metropolitan area study; a study of street and highway needs. Prepared for the State of Illinois, Dept. of Public Works, Division of Highways, in cooperation with Madison County, St. Clair County and U.S. Dept. of Commerce, Bureau of Public Roads.   Chicago, 1964-
       v. illus. (part col.) maps (part col.)
28 cm.
      Bibliography: v.1, leaves 68-69;
      I.Illinois. Division of Highways.
IU   NUC66-86325

Card 378

67-B. Foreign abbreviations.

    When the abbreviation of a foreign word is the first element in a name or in such a position that will be involved in the filing of the heading use the full form of the word, when known, instead of the abbreviation. If both the abbreviation and the full form of the word are the same as in English, however, keep the abbreviation.

67-C. Numerals.

    When a numeral occurs at the beginning of a corporate name in a foreign language, or in a position that will be involved in the alphabetic filing of the heading, then the numeral should be replaced by the work for that numeral in the vernacular.

68. <u>Changes of name</u>.

If the name of a corporate body changes, a new heading should be established for the new name and used for
cataloging all materials published under the new name. In
cataloging materials of a corporate body that has changed
names, the name used should be that of the body at the time
of the publication of the materials which may or may not
be the same name that is in current use.

The example given is that of Pennsylvania State
University which had various names prior to 1953 when its
present name was established. The heading used for cataloging publications of this institution depends on the
name in use at the time of publication. To catalog a publication which appeared before 1862, the proper heading
would be "Farmer's High School"; and those which appeared
between 1862 and 1874 would be entered under "Agricultural
College of Pennsylvania". Publications which came out
between 1874 and 1953 would be under the heading "Pennsylvania State College"; and everything published since 1953
would be under "Pennsylvania State University".

SUBORDINATE AND RELATED BODIES

A "subordinate body" is properly defined as one that
is subject to or under the authority of a superior corporate
body, and normally will be dependent on the higher body.
For the purpose of these rules, boards, trustees and other
governing bodies are treated as subordinate elements of the
corporate bodies they govern.

Subordinate bodies which have non-distinctive names
and are dependent on the names of higher bodies for their
identification or contain elements in their names which
imply subordination should be entered as a subheading under
a higher body.

Subordinate bodies which have distinctive names and
are not dependent on the names of higher bodies for identification and contain no element in their names which imply
subordination should be entered according to the general
rules for corporate bodies, 60-68.

Any subordinate body which can be classified as one
of the following types should be entered as a subheading
under a higher body.

Type 1. A name that includes the <u>entire</u> name of the
higher body. Omit the names of the higher body
in the subheading.

Brown University. *Library.*
    William Morris and the Kelmscott Press; an exhibition
held in the Library of Brown University, Providence, Rhode
Island, from October 9 to December 31, 1959. To which is
appended an address by Philip C. Duschnes before the
friends of the Library of Brown University, December 7,
1959. Providence, 1960.

    iii, 49 p. 16 plates (incl. facsims.) 27 cm.

Card
379

University of Connecticut. **Museum of Art.**
    The paintings of Charles Hawthorne. ₍Introd. by Marvin
S. Sadik, director. Storrs, Conn.₎ 1968.

    ₍88₎ p. illus. (1 col.), ports. 28 cm.

    Catalogue of an exhibition held at the University of Connecticut
Museum of Art, Storrs, Oct. 12–Nov. 17, 1968; Hirschl & Adler Galleries, New York, Dec. 5–31, 1968.

Card
380

University of North Carolina. **Trustees.**
    Academic freedom; laws, policies and regula-
tions governing invitations to and appearances of
visiting speakers affected by General statutes
116-199 and 200.   Chapel Hill, 1966.
    5 p. 28 cm.

Card
381

Yale University. *Library.*
    The Plato manuscripts; a new index. Prepared by the
Plato microfilm project of the Yale University Library
under the direction of Robert S. Brumbaugh and Rulon
Wells. New Haven, Yale University Press, 1968.

    vii, 163 p. 26 cm. $6.00

    "₍Index₎ provides listings of all the manuscript material held by
various libraries throughout the world, arranged in separate indexes
by location and by dialogue."
    Bibliography: p. 163.

    1. Plato—Manuscripts—Bibl. 2. Microfilms—Catalogs. I. Brum-
baugh, Robert Sherrick, 1918–   ed. II. Wells, Rulon, ed. III.
Title.

Z6616.P57Y35   016.184   68–13898

Library of Congress   ₍3₎

Card
382

Type 2. A name that contains a term that by definition indicates that it is a component part of a higher body, e.g. department, division, section, branch, unit, chapter, etc.

American Bankers Association. *Marketing Dept.*
    A selective, annotated bank marketing bibliography.
New York [1968]

   vii, 103 p. 28 cm.

Card
383

Bell and Howell Company. *Micro Photo Division.*
    Out-of-print books from the John G. White Folklore Collection at the Cleveland Public Library, reproduced by the duopage process by Micro Photo Division, Bell & Howell Co. Cleveland, 1966.

   321 p. 35 cm.

Card
384

British Museum. Dept. of Printed Books.
    Subject index of the modern books acquired
by the British Museum in the years 1916-1920,
other than those relating to the European War.
London, H. Pordes, 1965.
    1012 p. 24 cm.

Card
385

Enjay Chemical Company. Industrial Chemicals
Division.
    Ketones: acetone, methyl ethyl ketone
(MEK), methyl isobutyl ketone (MIBK).   [New
York, 1962]
    59 p. illus. 28 cm.

Card
386

Tennessee Valley Authority. *Division of Forestry Development.*
    Development of forests-fish-wildlife in the Tennessee Valley. [Norris, Tenn.] 1962.

   42 p. illus., maps. 28 cm.

   Cover title.
   Bibliography: p. 42.

   1. Forests and forestry—Tennessee Valley. 2. Wild life, Conservation of—Tennessee Valley. I. Title.

SD144.A17A54   62-64886

Library of Congress   [2]

Card
387

Type 3. A name that contains a word ordinarily implying administrative subordination, e.g. committee. There are bodies that have a name which contains a word that usually implies administrative subordination but are not subordinate to any other body, and there are others that are established to function as independent bodies and are not to be regarded as subordinate to any other body.

American Jewish Congress. Commission on Law and Social Action.
  Report on twenty state anti-discrimination agencies and the laws they administer.
New York, 1961.

Card 388

Council of Europe. Council for Cultural Co-operation.
    The teaching of chemistry at university level.
A report presented by Mr. Guy Ourisson .
Strasbourg, 1966.

Card 389

Card 390

Library Association. County Libraries Group.
    Readers' guide to books on choice of careers.
6th ed.   ⌈London⌉ 1966.

National Education Association of the United States. National Commission on Professional Rights and Responsibilities.
    Waterbury, Connecticut; a study of the inhibiting effect of political control on the quality of education.   ⌈Washington⌉ 1963.

Card 391

Young Men's Christian Associations. *National Campcraft Commission.*
    Handbook of trail campcraft, step-by-step guide; edited by John A. Ledlie. New York, Association Press ⌈1954⌉

    187 p. illus. 23 cm.
    Includes bibliography.

Card 392

    1. Camping.   I. Ledlie, John Andrew, 1898–   ed. II. Title:
    Trail campcraft.   III. Title.

    SK601.Y63   796.54   54—12613 ‡

    Library of Congress   ⌈55k10⌉

Type 4.   A name of a university, school or college that
simply indicates a particular field of study.

University of North Carolina.   School
of Journalism.
Responsibilities of journalism. Proceedings
of the dedicatory ceremonies for Howell Hall
as the new home of the School of Journalism,
the University of North Carolina, Chapel Hill,
October 21, 1960. Foreword by Norval Neil
Luxon.   ₍Chapel Hill, N.C., 1960₎
69 p. 23 cm.

Card
393

University of Wisconsin.   Library School.
Professional librarians; an inventory of
personnel and personnel needs in Wisconsin in
college, university, school, public and special
libraries.   Madison, 1965.
29 l. illus. 28 cm.

Card
394

Universidad Nacional (Argentina)
Facultad de Arquitectura y
Urbanismo. Biblioteca.
Normas para la catalogación de diapositivas.   ₍Buenos
Aires₎ 1967.

15 p. Illus. 23 cm.

(LACAP 68-2343)

Card
395

Université libre de Bruxelles. Institut
de sociologie.
Les régions du Borinage et du Centre à
l'heure de la Reconversion; XXIXe Semaine
sociale universitaire du 6 au 10 novembre 1961.
₍Brussels, 1962₎
464 p. illus. 24 cm.
Summaries in English.

Card
396

Type 5. A name that is <u>entirely</u> descriptive of the body's functions and that has a character that is common to the names of both subordinate bodies and independent bodies, e.g. institutes, centers, laboratories. In other words, those bodies which do not have a distinctive name normally will have to be entered as a subheading under a higher body.

Boston University. *African Studies Program.*
　　Selected African bibliographies: Cameroun, Gabon, Ivory Coast, Morocco, Rwanda and Burundi ₁and₁ Tunisia. Prepared for the Agency for International Development ₁by Édouard Bustin, Elaine Hagopian, and John Sommer. Boston₁ 1964.
　　　1 v. (various pagings)　28 cm.

Card 397

College Placement Council. *Research Information Center.*
　　A bibliography of selected research and statistical studies pertaining to college-trained manpower, 1960–66. ₁Bethlehem, Pa.₁ College Placement Council ₁1967₁
　　　58 p.　23 cm.

Card 398

Council of Europe.　Library and Documentation Centre.
　　List of European and North American periodicals dealing with questions concerning regional economy and planning and local administration. Strasbourg, 1963.

Card 399

Organization for Economic Co-operation and Development.
Directorate for Scientific Affairs.
　　Educational policy and planning: Austria.　Paris, O. E. C. D., 1968.

Card 400

Scripps Institution of Oceanography.
　　Marine Physical Laboratory.
　　Preliminary sea tests of snap-on cable fairings, ₁by₁ Michael S. Loughridge. ₁n. p. ₁ 1964.
　　　3 p. illus. (Its MPL Technical memorandum no. 144)

Card 401

Type 6. Any name that is so general that the name of a higher body is required for its identification.

American Association for Health, Physical Education and Recreation. Research Council.
    Softball for boys: skills test manual ₍by₎ David K. Brace, test consultant. ₍Washington, c1966₎
      44 p. illus. 24 cm. (AAHPER sports skills tests)

Card 402

Eastman Kodak Company. Research Library.
    Current subscription list. Rochester ₍N.Y.₎ Dept. of Information Services, Kodak Research Laboratories ₍1963₎
     ₍24₎ p. 28 cm.

Card 403

National Geographic Society, *Book Service.*
    Greece and Rome; builders of our world. ₍Washington₎ National Geographic Society ₍1968₎

    448 p. illus. (part col.), col. maps (1 fold. in pocket), ports. (part col.) 26 cm. (Story of man library) $11.95

Card 404

Northwestern University. Technological Institute.
    Fox River diversion scheme; senior design project of the class of 1965. Evanston, Ill., 1965.
      1 v. (various pagings) illus., tables, maps

Card 405

University of New Mexico. Art Gallery.
    The painter and the photograph; an exhibition, organized by the staff of the Art Gallery, the University of New Mexico, and shown during 1964 and 1965 at the following institutions: Rose Art Museum, Brandeis University, Waltham, Mass. ₍and others₎ Van Deren Coke ₍director of the exhibition. 1st ed. Albuquerque₎ University of New Mexico Press ₍1964₎

    79 p. illus. 26 cm.

    1. Art and photography. 2. Paintings — Exhibitions. 3. Photography — Exhibitions. I. Coke, Van Deren, 1921—

Card 406

69-A. Direct or Indirect subheading.

        In the chain of hierarchy of corporate bodies it is
common to find bodies which are subordinate to a higher body
which in turn is subordinate to another body, etc. until
the end is reached with the highest body to which all are
subordinate.

        To establish a subheading it is necessary to deter-
mine which of the elements in the chain of hierarchy are
essential to clarify the function and/or the identity of
the lowest body as an element of the highest body. The
elements which are deemed essential are retained in the
establishment of the heading, the others are eliminated.

69-A-1. Direct subheading.

        Hierarchy: General Electric Company.
                    Atomic Products Division.
                    Aircraft Nuclear Propulsion Department.

        The heading established for the "Aircraft Nuclear
Propulsion Department" does not need to include the middle
element, "Atomic Products Division" to clarify the function
or to identify the "Aircraft Nuclear Propulsion Dept." The
heading will be:

        General Electric Company. Aircraft Nuclear
            Propulsion Department.

Also, as no other division of General Electric will have an
"Aircraft Nuclear Propulsion Dept." it is and will most
likely continue to be the only such department in the entire
company.

69-A-2. Indirect subheading.

        Hierarchy: University of North Carolina
                    Division of Health Affairs
                    Program Planning Section

        In this case the heading must consist of all three
elements because it would not be clear that the "Program
Planning Section" is part of the "Division of Health Affairs".
If "Division of Health Affiars" was omitted, then it would
appear that the "Program Planning Section" was a subordinate
body which planned programs of the entire university and not
just of the "Division of Health Services." The heading will
be:
        University of North Carolina. Division of Health
            Affairs. Program Planning Section.

70.   Other subordinate bodies.

This rule is redundant to what already has been stated in rule 69; i.e. a subordinate body is entered directly under its own name if its name does not belong to one of the six types described in rule 69. In those cases where the subordinate body cannot be categorized into any of those six types then the general rules for corporate bodies (rules 60-68) should be applied.

71.   Related bodies.

71-A.   General rule.

Any corporate body, such as a society, association, auxiliary, or any other which is closely related to, but yet not subordinate to, another body should be entered as a subheading under the heading for the body to which it is related if: (1) its name contains the entire name of the body to which it is related, either internally or at the end; or (2) its name is insufficient for identification without the addition of that body's name; or (3) its name is normally used only in association with that name.   If the name of the body to which it is related occurs in its name, omit that part of the name form the subheading if grammatically permissible.

However, if it is uncertain what the relationship is and one body might be subordinate to another body, then treat the body as subordinate under the provisions of rules 69 and 70.

CHAPTER VII

GOVERNMENT BODIES AND OFFICIALS
Rules 78-81

The cataloging of materials produced by government bodies and agencies is basically the same as that of other corporate bodies. There are some bodies subordinate to others which are treated as independent bodies, and others which must be entered as subheadings under higher bodies. But, due to the very complexity and uniqueness of the organization and functions of governments it is necessary to establish special rules. The word "government" as used in these rules refers to all levels of government, not just national governments.

As stated in the introductory note in the AACR those agencies which help carry out the basic legislative, judicial and executive functions of government are entered as subheadings under the heading established for the government. All other agencies and bodies of a government are to be entered under their own names, if possible. This phrase "if possible" means that in the following rules there are guidelines to follow in order to determine which agencies can be entered under their own names and which have to be entered as subheadings. The most reliable source for helping to determine the correct entry for U.S. government bodies and agencies is the current issue of the annual publication, "U.S. government organization manual."

78. General rule.

78-A. A corporate body created and/or controlled by a government should be entered according to the general rules for corporate bodies (rules 60-71) if it is one of the following seven types, regardless of its official nature (except for necessary references) or whether or not it is subordinate to an agency of government.

However, before applying any general rule for corporate bodies the exceptions in the paragraphs that follow the seven types should be checked.

Any governmental body or agency that can be classified as one of the seven types and is not excluded due to the exceptions that follow the seven types is to be treated according to the provisions of the general rules for corporate bodies, i.e. rules 60-71.

A governmental body or agency that cannot be classified as one of the seven types, or if there is doubt that it is one, or is excluded due to the exceptions that follow the seven types is to be treated under the provisions of rule 78-B. See the appendices for lists of U.S. and British government agencies determined by the rules for government bodies and agencies.

Type 1. Organizations engaged in commercial, cultural, or scientific activities, or the promotion of such activities. Exception: Bodies designated by terms that are commonly used in the particular country to denote administrative agencies of government, e.g. in American usage, "bureau", "administration", "service", "agency", etc. In case of doubt concerning usage, however, this exception does not apply. (This exception was added by the Library of Congress after publication. The British Cataloguing Rules Sub-Committee has not accepted this exception and so differences will occur in certain entries until an agreement is reached.)

Examples:

   British text
      Environmental Science Services Administration
      Maritime Administration
      National Aeronautics and Space Administration
      Soil Conservation Service

   North American text
      U.S. Environmental Science Services Administration
      U.S. Maritime Administration
      U.S. National Aeronautics and Space Administration
      U.S. Soil Conservation Service.

It is very curious to note that when terms denoting administrative agencies such as "administration" and "service" are used in the name of corporate bodies that fall into Type 1, they must be entered as a subheading under the name of the government, but when these same terms are used for corporate bodies that can be categorized in types 2 through 7, then they can be entered directly under their own names, that is, of course, when one follows the exception devised by the Library of Congress and appended to Type 1.

Geological Survey.
Water wells and springs in Borrego, Carrizo, and San Felipe Valley areas, San Diego and Imperial Counties, California. ₁Sacramento, California Dept. of Water Resources₁ 1968.

1 v. (various pagings) maps (2 fold. in pocket) 28 cm. (California. Dept. of Water Resources. Bulletin no. 91–15)

Card
407

Geological Survey. (North Dakota)
Generalized glacial map of North Dakota.
₁Bismarck? 1965?₁
col. map 15 x 25 cm.

Card
408

National Institutes of Health.
Scientific and technical information activities of the National Institutes of Health, fiscal year 1963. ₁Washington, D.C.₁ U.S. Public Health Service, 1964.
1 v. (various paging) 27 cm.

Card
409

National Oceanographic Data Center.
Introduction to the National Oceanographic Data Center. Washington, Available on request from the National Oceanographic Data Center and the U.S. Naval Oceanographic Office, 1963.
vi, 11 p. illus.. fold. chart. 27 cm.

Card
410

National Youth Employment Council.
The work of the Youth Employment Service 1965–1968: a report. London, H. M. S. O., 1968.

ix, 62 p. 2 illus. 25 cm. 6/6

Card
411

Warren Spring Laboratory.
Individual factors that affect behavioral efficiency - anxiety, 1958-1961. Stevenage, England, 1962.
₁10₁ l
1. Anxiety—Bibl. 2. Behaviorism (Psychology) —Bibl. I. Title.
InNd   NUC66-55422

Card
412

Type 1.   Exception.

U.S. Fish and Wildlife Service. 　　　Pelagic fur seal investigations, Alaska waters, 1962, by Clifford H. Fiscus, Gary A. Baines, and Ford Wilke. ₁n.p. ₁ 1964. 　　　59 p. illus. (Its Special Scientific report; fisheries, no. 475) 　　　Includes bibliography.	Card 413
U. S. Food and Drug Administration. 　　　Handling of food grains: the Food and Drug Administration's grain sanitation program. ₁Washington, U. S. Govt. Print. Off. , 1965₁ 　　　11 p. (Its Publication no. 29)	Card 414
U.S. Maritime Administration. 　　　Survey of the ports of Alaska. ₁Washington₁ 1965. 　　　iv, 102 p. illus. , maps.	Card 415
U.S. National Aeronautics and Space Administration. 　　　Electrical power management survey manual. Washington, 1965. 　　　iii, 31 p. tables. 27 cm. (Its NASA SP-6007)	Card 416
U.S. National Park Service. 　　　Chickamauga ₁and₁ Chattanooga National Military Park. Georgia - Tennessee. ₁Wash- ington, 1965₁ 　　　1 v. illus. 24 cm. 　　　1. Chickamauga and Chattanooga National Military Park. DI NUC66-91809	Card 417

Type 2. Institutions. (typically with their own physical plant)

The word "institutions" here refers mainly to those agencies of governments such as schools, libraries, museums, hospitals, laboratories and other such bodies which usually have their own physical facilities.

Biblioteca Nacional (Brazil)
 Cinqüenta anos de biblioteconomia 1915–1965; exposição comemorativa do cinqüentenário dos cursos de biblioteconomia da Biblioteca Nacional. ₍Rio de Janeiro₎ Ministério da Educação e Cultura, 1965.
 17 p. port. 24 cm.

Card 418

British Museum. Dept. of Printed Books.
 Rules for compiling the catalogues of printed books, maps and music in the British Museum. Rev. ed. London, British Museum, printed by order of the Trustees, 1936 ₍1960₎
 67 p.

Card 419

Library of Congress.
 Poland in the collections of the Library of Congress; an overview, by Kazimierz Grzybowski. Washington; ₍For sale by the Supt. of Docs., U. S. Govt. Print. Off.₎ 1968 ₍i. e. 1969₎
 iii, 26 p. illus. 27 cm. 0.40

Card 420

National Gallery.
 Early Netherlandish school, by Martin Davies. 3rd ed. (revised). London, National Gallery, 1968.
 206 p. 25 cm. (*Its* Catalogues) 10/-

Card 421

National Portrait Gallery.
 This new man: a discourse in portraits. Edited by J. Benjamin Townsend and introd. by Charles Nagel. With an essay by Oscar Handlin. Washington, Published for the National Portrait Gallery by the Smithsonian Institution Press; ₍distributed by Random House, New York₎ 1968.
 217 p. ports. (part col.) 27 cm. (Smithsonian publication 4752) $6.95

 1. Portraits, American—Catalogs. 2. U. S.—Biog.—Portraits. I. Townsend, James Benjamin, 1918– II. Handlin, Oscar, 1915– III. Title. **(Series)**

N7593.N23   704.94′2′0973   68–8535

Library of Congress ₍3₎

Card 422

Type 3. Installations and parks.

     The term "installation" as used here refers to land and the improvements thereon which are devoted to military purposes, e.g. forts, training camps, air bases, etc. "Parks" includes all tracts of land kept for ornament and/or recreation, zoos, botanical gardens, as well as reserves, sanctuaries, and preserves which are maintained in their natural state for the preservation of plant and animal life, or for the conservation of natural beauty.

Griffis Air Force Base.
    Management projects.   Rome, N.Y.
/195-?7
    22p.   illus.

Card
423

New York Botanical Garden.
    Various ways in which material may be prepared for use in dried arrangements. New York, 1956.
    4 p.   36cm.

Card
424

Royal Botanic Garden, Edinburgh.
    The Royal Botanic Garden, Edinburgh; a brief descriptive and illustrated account.   Edinburgh, H.M. Stationery Office, 1957.
    52p.   illus.

Card
425

Royal Botanic Gardens, Kew.
    The Royal Botanic Gardens, Kew. Illustrated guide.   London, H.M. Stationery Office, 1951.
    134p.   illus.

Card
426

Type 4. Bodies created by intergovernmental agreement.

A body created by two or more governments which could not be entered under either one of the governments is entered under its own name. This is similar to rule 71-B on joint committees, commissions, etc.

Buffalo and Erie County Public Library.
Shaker literature in the rare book room of the Buffalo and Erie County Public Library. A bibliography compiled by Esther C. Winter and rev. by Joanna S. Ellett. Buffalo, 1967.

43 p. 23 cm. 2.00

Card 427

Council of Social Agencies of Rochester and Monroe County. Information-Service Dept.
Directory of health, welfare and recreation services, Rochester and Monroe County, N.Y. [Rev.] Rochester, N.Y. [foreword 1966]
vii, 236 p. 22 cm.

Card 428

Johnson-Wyandotte Regional Planning Commission.
Feasibility report on a unified sanitary sewer system for the Turkey Creek drainage area. [Kansas City, Mo.] Community Studies, 1959.
19 p. table, maps. 28 cm.

Card 429

State-Federal Crop and Livestock Reporting Service.
Minnesota's dairy industry.
St. Paul, 1965.
ii, 22p. maps.

Card 430

Twin Cities Metropolitan Planning Commission.
Metropolitan economic study.
St. Paul, 1960.
65p. illus. maps.

Card 431

Type 5. Authorities and trusts for the operation of
         utilities and industries.

As used here, the term "authority" should be defined
as a governmental agency which has the right to control,
command or determine; and a "trust" is defined as an industrial and/or commercial operation that controls completely
or almost completely the production of a certain commodity
or service.

Railways and Harbours Board.
    Report of the Railways and Harbours Board
relative to the construction of a new line of
railway between Hoedspruit and Phalaborwa
presented to both Houses of Parliament 1961.
Pretoria, Printed for the Govt. Print. by
Cape Times, 1961.
    2 v. in 1. map. 32 cm.

Card 432

Port of London Authority.
    Notes on the port of London. ₁London, 1965₁
    36 p. illus., fold. map. 25 cm.

Card 433

New York City Housing Authority.
    Fact sheet. ₁New York₁ 1966.
    64 p. 21 x 28 cm. illus.

Card 434

Leith Dock Commission.
    The port of Leith; its history and development,
together with information on its trade, facilities
for handling and distributing cargoes in and out,
schedules of rates, etc.   Edinburgh, Adcon, 1964.
    156 p. illus., maps (part fold., part col.)

Card 435

Atomic Energy Commission.
    Reading resources in atomic energy. ₁Oak Ridge, Tenn.₁
U. S. Atomic Energy Commission, Division of Technical
Information ₁1968₁

    iv, 20 p. 22 cm. (Understanding the atom)

    Cover title:

Card 436

    1. Atomic energy — Bibliography.   I. Title.   (Series: U. S.
Atomic Energy Commission. Understanding the atom)

Z5160.U56   016.5397   68–60542

Library of Congress   ₁2₁

Type 6. Banks, corporations, manufacturing plants, farms, and similar specific enterprises. Examples of some "similar specific enterprises" are: Alaska Railroad, Commodity Credit Corporation, and the Panama Canal Company.

Government Service Insurance System.
    Handbook of information on retirement insurance. ₁Manila₁ 1965.
      36 p. 34 cm.
    "Updated and reprinted from the GSIS handbook of information ... published in April, 1963."

Card 437

National Development Credit Agency (Tanganyika)
    ... Project agreement (agricultural credit project) between National development credit agency and International development association ... ₁Washington, D.C.₁ 1966.
      8 p. 27 cm. (Credit number 80 TA)
      1. Debts, Public–Tanganyika.   I. International Development Association.
    MH-L   NUC66-92303

Card 438

Type 7. Established churches.

This refers to a specific church or religion established by a government as its official one. As the U.S. has no official religion only foreign churches will be entered under this type.

Church of Scotland.
    The place of women in the church;
a study document. Edinburgh, Saint Andrew Press, 1959.
      40p. 22cm.

Card 439

There are exceptions to these seven types which are to be
treated according to rule 78-B.

Excepted from rule 78-A are bodies that are designated as ministries (in the U.S. the ministries are termed
"Departments" e.g. Department of Justice, Department of
Commerce, etc.) or by terms that by definition denote that
the body is a component part of something else, e.g. department, division, section, branch, bureau, and foreign equivalents. (Cf. rule 69, types 2 and 3).

Also excluded from rule 78-A are libraries, archives,
and other government bodies that normally function primarily
as service units of a particular agency of government if
their names contain the name of the agency as the sole identifying element or require the addition of the agency's
name for their identification. (Cf. rule 69, types 1,5 and
6)

California. Division of Highways.
      General specifications for relocation or demo-
lition and removal of improvements to clear
right of way. ₁Sacramento, 1965₁
      57 p. illus.
	Card
	440

Florida. Sheriff's Bureau.
      Florida Law Enforcement Academy. Florida
Sheriff's Memorial Training Center. Tallahas-
see ₁1963₁
      22 l. illus.
	Card
	441

Nigeria. Ministry of Economic Development.
      Federal government development programme,
1962-68. Lagos, Federal Printing Division
₁1962₁
            46 p. tables. (Sessional paper no. 1 of 1962)
      Cover title.
      1. Nigeria—Economic policy.   I. Title.
MiEM   NUC66-94653
	Card
	442

Singapore. Ministry of Culture.
　　　Separation; Singapore's separation from
the Federation of Malaysia 9th August, 1965.
ₗSingapore, 1965ₗ
　　　65 p. illus. 19 cm.

Card
443

Spain. Ministerio de Información y Turismo.
　　　Spain. ₗMadrid, 1962ₗ
　　　290 p. col. illus., 69 col. plates, ports.,
maps. 22 cm.

Card
444

U. S. *Dept. of Health, Education, and Welfare. Library.*
　　　Community planning for health, education, and welfare;
an annotated bibliography. Compiled for the Bureau of
Family Services ₗby Dorothy M. Jonesₗ Washington, U. S.
Bureau of Family Services; ₗfor sale by the Supt. of Docs.,
U. S. Govt. Print. Off., 1967ₗ
　　　viii, 57 p. 23 cm. 0.25

Card
445

U. S. *Dept. of the Interior.*
　　　Surface mining and our environment; a special report to
the Nation. ₗWashington, For sale by the Sup'. of Docs.
U. S. Govt. Print. Off., 1967ₗ

　　　124 p. col. illus., col. maps. 31 cm.

Card
446

U. S. United States Savings Bonds Division.
　　　Some legal aspects of United States savings
bonds. Washington, U.S. Govt. Print. Off.
ₗ1965ₗ
　　　11 p. (SBD-757-5)

Card
447

Zambia. Ministry of Commerce and Industry.
　　　Outline of the government's industrial policy.
First published 10th October, 1964. Revised
and re-issued 3rd January, 1966. Lusaka,
1966.
　　　10 p.
　　　1. Economic development—Zambia.
MBU　　　　　　　　　　　NUC67-2798

Card
448

78-B. Any government body which cannot be classified into any of the seven types must be entered as a subheading under the heading for the government and in accordance with the provisions of rules.79-86.

Ghana. *Administrative Committee on Matters Connected with the Revision of Salaries and Wages, 1957.*
Report. Accra, Govt. Printer ₁1958₁

viii, 59 p. 25 cm.

Card 449

New Zealand. Workers' Compensation Board.
The Workers' Compensation Act, 1956, and amendments; a brief guide. Prepared by Ian B. Campbell, secretary. 7th ed. ₁Wellington, N. Z., 1965₁
56 p. 16 cm.

Card 450

South Africa. Office of Census and Statistics.
A survey of the accounts of public and other companies for the years 1961-62 and 1960-61. Pretoria, Govt. Printer ₁1963₁
44 p. tables. 33 cm. (Its National accounts and finance. Memorandum no. 33)

Card 451

U. S. *General Accounting Office.*
Unnecessary costs incurred for temporary storage of household goods for military personnel, Department of Defense; report to the Congress of the United States by the Comptroller General of the United States. ₁Washington₁ 1963.

2 1., 17 p. 27 cm.

Card 452

U.S. General Services Administration.
Techniques of day-to-day supervision.
Washington, Office of Industrial Resources, International Cooperation Administration, 1958 ₁
cover-title, 17 p. (₁U.S. ₁ International Cooperation Administration. Technical bulletin no. 53)
Reprint.
1.Supervisors. I.Title. (Series: U.S. Agency for International Development. Technical bulletin no. 53)
DPAHO

NUC67-2091

Card 453

79. <u>Subordinate agencies and units.</u>   (Cf. rule 69-A)

79-A. Direct subheading. A government body or agency that is to be entered under the name of the government because of the exceptions of 78-A and/or 78-B and which is also subordinate to another such body should be treated as a direct subheading under the name of the government if its name has not been or is not likely to be used by another body in the same jurisdiction. In other words, if it is unique in the government and no other subagency could be confused with it. A subagency with a name such as, "Bureau of the Census" is unique, but "Office of Personnel" occurs in many governmental agencies and therefore has to be entered as an indirect subheading as illustrated under 79-B.

U. S. *Bureau of the Census.*
    Housing construction statistics, 1889 to 1964. Washington, For sale by the Superintendent of Documents, U. S. Govt. Print. Off., 1966,
      v. 805 p. illus., maps. 30 cm.

Card
454

U.S. Office of Naval Operations.
    The effects of radiation on populations.
[Washington] 1958-60.
    2 v. in 1. illus. (Its OEG report, 78)

Card
455

U. S. Public Health Service.
    Grants for training projects; policy statement.   [Washington] 1965.
      vi, 21 p. 22 cm. (Its Publication no. 1302)

Card
456

U.S. Wage and Hour and Public Contracts
    Divisions.
    Wholesale trade; a study to evaluate the minimum wage and maximum hours standards of the Fair labor standards act.   [Washington] 1965.
      vii, 12, A-48 p. illus.
      Cover title.
    On cover: Report submitted to the Congress in accordance with the requirements of section 4(d) of the Fair labor standards act.
    MH-BA   NUC66-91374

Card
457

79-B. Indirect subheadings. A body which cannot be entered as a direct subheading should be treated as a subheading under the lowest element of the hierarchy that can be entered directly under the name of the government. Any agency in the hierarchy that is not or is not likely to be essential to distinguish bodies with the same name or to identify the body should be omitted.

Kentucky. *Dept. of Education. Bureau of Administration and Finance.*
Pupil transportation: growth and final calculation. ₍Frankfort₎ 1967.

iv, 18 p. illus. 27 cm.

Card 458

North Carolina. Dept. of Conservation and Development. Travel and Promotion Division.
Hunting in North Carolina. Raleigh ₍1966₎
13 p. map. 28 cm.

Card 459

Uganda. Ministry of Planning and Community Development. Statistics Branch.
The patterns of income, expenditure and consumption of African unskilled workers in Kampala, February 1964. ₍Entebbe₎ 1965.
16, ₍26₎ p. 32 cm.

Card 460

U. S. *Dept. of the Interior. Office of Oil and Gas.*
Plain facts about oil. ₍Washington₎ 1962.

51 p. illus. 27 cm.

Card 461

U. S. *Dept. of Veterans Benefits. Guardianship Service.*
Training guide for accounts analyst guardianship program. Washington, 1962.

15 p. 25 cm. (₍U. S.₎ Veterans Administration. TG27-3)

Card 462

1. U. S. Dept. of Veterans Benefits. Guardianship Service—Accounting. 2. Pensions, Military—U. S. 3. Veterans—U. S. 4. Guardian and ward—U. S. ɪ. Title.

UB357.A27 TG27-3   62-64799 ‡

Library of Congress   ₍2₎

80. Government officials.

80-A. Chiefs of state, etc.

The headings for presidents, governors, sovereigns, chiefs of state, etc. can be made either under the name of the office he holds or under his personal name. Works which can be attributed to chiefs of state, etc. are divided into two groups, (1) official communications and (2) other speeches and writings. The provisions of rule 17-C are used to determine if the entry is made under the corporate heading for the office he holds or as a work of personal authorship.

California. Governor, 1959-1967
     (Brown)
     Recreation policy of the state of California, with an analysis of the State's recreation problem and its solution, with a program to implement the policy. Sacramento, 1962.
     23p. illus.

Card 463

Venezuela. President, 1959-1964
     (Betancourt)
     Toward a healthier economy; address delivered before the National Congress of Venezuela, May 5, 1961. Caracas, 1961.
     12p.

Card 464

U. S. *President, 1963-1969 (Lyndon B. Johnson)*
     Welfare of children; message from the President of the United States transmitting recommendations for the welfare of children. [Washington, U. S. Govt. Print. Off., 1967]

12 p. 24 cm. (90th Congress, 1st session. House of Representatives. Document no. 54)

Caption title.

1. Child welfare—U. S. I. Title. (Series: U. S. 90th Congress, 1st session, 1967. House. Document no. 54)

HV741.A438   362.7'0973   67-61268

Library of Congress   [3]

Card 465

80-B. Heads of government.

For those who are not also chiefs of state in their official capacities, the heading consists of his title or of the title of his office as a subheading under the name of the government. The title used should be according to the usage found on the publications. No dates or names are included in the subheading as is done for chiefs of state.

New York (City) Mayor.
An action program for the aged in New York City; a report to the people of New York City by Mayor Robert F. Wagner. New York, 1960.
24p. illus.

Card
466

Philadelphia. Mayor.
The road ahead; a message on the state of the city. Delivered before the Council of the City of Philadelphia, March 22, 1956.
Philadelphia, 1956.
16p.

Card
467

Gt. Brit. Prime Minister.
The economic implications of full employment. London, H. M. Stationery Off., 1956.
13p.

Card
468

Vietnam (Democratic Republic, 1946-   )
Prime Minister.
Text of report by North Vietnamese Premier Van Dong to National Assembly on 16 April 1966. [Washington] 1966.
43 p. 27 cm. (Foreign Broadcast Information Service. Daily report. Far East. Suppl. no. 84. 1966)
1. Vietnam (Democratic Republic, 1946-   )—Pol. & govt.   I. Pham-van-Dong, 1906-   II. Title.
CSt-H   NUC67-823

Card
469

80-D.   Other officials.

The heading for any other government official consists only of the name of the body or agency that he represents, and not his title.

U. S. *General Accounting Office.*
Review of financial and administrative activities relating
to the development and construction of the Dulles International Airport, Federal Aviation Agency, September
1961; report to the Congress of the United States by the
Comptroller General of the United States. Washington,
1962.

129 l.   illus.   27 cm.

Card
470

U.S.   Dept. of Justice.
Review of voluntary agreements
program under the Defense Production
Act; report by the Attorney General.
Washington, U.S. Govt. Print. Off.,
1957.
v, 45p.

Card
471

But, if the official is not a part of any agency of
government, or if he is part of one that has no name but
that of the official, the heading consists of his title as
a subheading under the government.

Los Angeles Co.   County Clerk.
Manual of civil procedure for
use of superior court clerks.
3 rev. ed.   Los Angeles, 1962.
1 v. (loose-leaf)

Card
472

U.S.   Architect of the Capitol.
The prayer room in the United
States Capitol. Washington, U.S.
Govt. Print. Off., 1956.
8 p.   illus.

Card
473

81. Legislative bodies.

81-A. If a legislative body has more than one chamber, each one should be entered as a subheading under the name of the legislature.

California. *Legislature. Assembly. Legislative Reference Service.*
Bibliography of the California **Legislature. Prepared at** the request of the Assembly Committee on **Elections and** Reapportionment. Sacramento, 1965.

19 l. 28 cm.

Card 474

California. Legislature. Senate. Fact-Finding Committee on Agriculture.
Report on pesticides.   [Sacramento] Senate of the State of California, 1965.
91 p. 23 cm.

Card 475

U.S. Congress. House.
Documentary history of the construction and development of the United States Capitol Building and Grounds. Washington, U.S. Govt. Print. Off., 1960.
ii, 26p.

Card 476

U.S. Congress. Senate.
Tributes to Richard M. Nixon, Vice President of the United States. Remarks delivered in the United States Senate on January 17, 1961. Washington, U.S. Govt. Print. Off., 1961.
ii, 30p.

Card 477

81-B. Committees and other subordinate units should be entered as subheadings under the legislative body or of a particular chamber, as each case dictates. Do not include in these headings the dates or numbers of particular sessions of the legislative body.

U. S. *Congress. House. Committee on Science and Astronautics.*
Memorial to Dr. Robert H. Goddard. Hearing, Eighty-ninth Congress, first session, on H. J. Res. 597. September 7, 1965. Washington, U. S. Govt. Print. Off., 1965.

iii, 24 p. 24 cm.

Card 478

U. S. *Congress. House. Committee on Interstate and Foreign Commerce. Subcommittee on Public Health and Welfare.*
Medical library assistance. Hearing, Ninety-first Congress, first session on H. R. 11223, a bill to amend the Public health service act to extend for three years the programs of assistance for medical libraries. May 22, 1969. Washington, U. S. Govt. Print. Off., 1969.

iii, 145 p. 24 cm.

Card 479

U. S. *Congress. Senate. Committee on Armed Services.*
Military cold war education and speech review policies. Hearings before the Special Preparedness Subcommittee of the Committee on Armed Services, United States Senate, Eighty-seventh Congress, second session ... Washington, U. S. Govt. Print. Off., 1962–

pts. illus. 24 cm.

Hearings held Jan. 23   1962–

Card 480

U. S. *Congress. Senate. Committee on Public Works. Subcommittee on Air and Water Pollution.*
Waste management research and environmental quality management. Hearings, Ninetieth Congress, second session ... Washington, U. S. Govt. Print. Off., 1968.

iv, 451, x p. illus. 24 cm.

Hearings held May 22–July 10, 1968.
Bibliography: p. 261–262.

1. Pollution—U. S.   I. Title.

TD180.U54   628'.54   68–62895

Library of Congress   ₍3₎

Card 481

U. S. *Congress. Joint Committee on Printing.*
Report of a study of the Federal printing program.
₁Washington, 1966₁

iv, 36, A327 p. fold. maps. 22 x 28 cm.

At head of title: 89th Congress, 2d session. Joint committee print.

Card 482

1. Printing, Public—U. S.   I. Title.   II. Title: Federal printing program.

JK1685.A1A5   655.5′95′097?   77–6120
                                           MARC

Library of Congress   69 ₍2₎

81-C. When a heading is to be established for a particular legislature as a whole or for one of its chambers as whole be sure to include the year or years and the number if the successive legislatures are numbered consecutively. If in such cases numbered sessions are also involved, be sure to give the session and its number, following the name and number of the legislature, and add the year or years of the session.

U. S. *90th Congress. 2d session, 1968.*
Memorial addresses and eulogies in the Congress of the United States on the life and contributions of Hubert Baxter Scudder. Washington, U. S. Govt. Print. Off., 1968.

v, 11 p. port. 24 cm. (*Its* House document no. 400)

Card 483

U. S. *91st Congress, 1st session, 1969.*
Memorial services held in the House of Representatives and Senate of the United States, together with remarks presented in eulogy of Robert A. Everett, late a Representative from Tennessee, Ninety-first Congress, first session. Washington, U. S. Govt. Print. Off., 1969.

v, 88 p. port. 24 cm.

Card 484

1. Everett, Robert A., 1915–1969.   I. Title.

JK1030.E94U5   328.73′0924   [B]   74–602740
                                                MARC

Library of Congress   69 ₍3₎

CHAPTER VIII

EXCEPTIONS FOR ENTRY UNDER PLACE -- Rules 98 and 99

The major differences between the North American text and the British text are in the rules 98 and 99 of the North American text. Rule 98 on local churches, as it appears in the North American text, is based on the ALA rule for entering a church under the name of the city in which it is located. It is quite unlike the rule for local churches in the British text.

There is no rule 99, or even anything vaguely resembling it, in the British text. This rule was added to the North American text under the pretense that large research libraries in the United States could not afford to adapt their catalogs to the provisions of the general rules for corporate bodies. That pretext was given even in view of the fact that large research libraries in Great Britain and New Zealand were adapting to the new rules.

98. Local churches, etc.

The rule for local churches, cathedrals, monasteries, temples, mosques, etc. was completely rewritten for the North American text. There is no reason why a church cannot be entered under its own name just as any other type of corporate body is entered under its own name.

The following rule for local churches, cathedrals, monasteries, temples, mosques, etc. is from the British text, and is the one that should be used.

A. General rule. Enter a local church, cathedral, monastery, convent, abbey, temple, mosque, or the like, in accordance with general rules 60-64. If, however, variant forms of the body appear in formal presentations of the name in the body's own publications, enter under the predominant form. If no one form predominates, choose a form according to the following order of preference:

1) a name beginning with, or consisting of, the name of the person, persons, object, place, or event to which the church, etc., is dedicated, or after which it is named:

2) a name beginning with a generic word or phrase descriptive of a type of church, etc.;

3) a name beginning with the name of the location in which the church, etc., is situated.

B. <u>Additions to names</u>. Add to a name chosen according to the preferences listed in A above the name of the parish and/or other location in which the church, etc., is situated, as and where appropriate.

> St Clement's Church, Leigh-on-Sea
> xParish Church of St Clement
> xLeigh Church
> xLeigh-on-Sea Parish Church
> St James, Louth
> xLouth Parish Church
> St. Katherine Cree Church, Lodon
> St. Lawrence Jewry, London
> St. Nicholas Church, Pevensey
> xPevensey Parish Church
> All Saints Church, Birchington
> Epiphany Evangelical Lutheran Church, Eau Claire, Wis.
> xEvangelical Church of Eau Claire
> Visitation Monastery, Waldron
> xMonastery of the Visitation, Waldron
> Vistation Monastery, Walmer
> xMonastery of the Visitation, Walmer
>
> Church of St Thomas the Apostle, Winchelsea
> xWinchelsea Church ·
> Church of the English Martyrs, Sparkhill
> Collegiate Church of the Holy Trinity, Tattershall
> Minster Church of the Blessed Virgin Mary, Ilminster
> Parish Church of Limpsfield
> Parish Church of St Peter, Chertsey
> xChertsey Parish Church
>
> Beechen Grove Baptist Church, Watford
> Tewkesbury Abbey

C. <u>Congregations, parishes, church societies, etc</u>. Enter a congregation, parish, church society, or other such group that is the corporate body holding worship in a church, according to the rules for local churches, A and B above.

> Anerley Society of the New Church
> English River Congregation of the Church of the Brethren

In some instances, however, a parish or society may be a corporate body distinct from but related to that of the church. Relate such bodies by "see also" references.

> First Church, New Haven
> xxFirst Ecclesiastical Society, New Haven
> First Ecclesiastical Society, New Haven
> xxFirst Church, New Haven
> St Albans Church, Washington, D. C.
> xxSt Albans Parish, Washington, D. C.
> St Albans Parish, Washington, D. C.
> xxSt Albans Church, Washington, D. C.

First Presbyterian Church, New York.
    Memorial of Rev. William W.
Phillips, D.D. Printed by request
of the session and of the Board of
Trustees of the First Presbyterian
Church. New York, Scribner, 1865.
    66p. illus.

Card
485

Reform Congregation Keneseth Israel,
        Philadelphia.
    90th anniversary record of the
Reform Congregation Keneseth Israel.
Philadelphia, Pomerantz, 1937.
    22p. illus.

Card
486

Riverside Church, New York.
    The Riverside Church in the city of
New York; a handbook of the institution
and its building. Philadelphia,
Franklin Printing Co., 1931.
    127p. illus.

Card
487

St. Bridget's Church, Cleveland.
    The prayer-book of St. Bridget's
parish. Cleveland, McBride & Co.,
1901.
    iii, 264p.

Card
488

Twelfth Baptist Church, Boston.
    One hundred and five years by
faith; a history of the Twelfth
Baptist Church, Boston. Rev.
William H. Hester, D.D., Pastor.
Boston, 1946.
    141p. illus.

Card
489

99. Certain other corporate bodies.

This rule was fabricated to keep content those librarians who are fearful of change. To append rule 99 to the chapter on headings for corporate bodies is comparable to saying, "What was good enough for my forefathers is good enough for me".

The argument often heard against using such headings as, "University of Kansas" instead of the awkward and unrealistic, "Kansas. University" is that it would place many entries under the word "university". However, in reality it would be better to have a group of entries under the word "university" than to compound the problems created by having so many corporate entries under such names as Kansas, New York, etc.

Entry under place was widely used in the old ALA rules and to perpetuate such impractical headings is inexcusable. The whole purpose of a card catalog is to facilitate, and not to hinder the public in determining if the library has certain materials.

The British text contains no such rule for arbitrarily entering certain corporate bodies under place. All corporate bodies are entered according to the other rules in the chapter on headings for corporate bodies. It is strongly urged that rule 99 be completely disregarded, as there are indications that this adjunct probably will be eliminated from the next edition of the North American text.

Carnegie Library of Pittsburgh.
  The Pilgrims; selected material
for use in connection with the
Pilgrim Tercentenary Celebration.
Pittsburgh, 1920.
  13p.

Card 490

Library Company of Philadelphia.
  The original articles of
association of the Library Company
of Philadelphia. Now first printed,
together with the charter, etc., etc.
Philadelphia, Collins, printer, 1864.
  20p.

Card 491

State University of New York at Buffalo.
Dept. of Mechanical Engineering.
Studies of two-dimensional flow in a curved
channel by Robert P. Apmann ₍and others₎
Buffalo, State University of New York, c1965.
1 v. (various pagings) diagrs. (State
University of New York at Buffalo. School of
Engineering. Dept. of Mechanical Engineering.

Card
492

University of California, Los Angeles.
Center of Latin American Studies.
Communism in Latin America, a bibliography; the post-
war years (1945–1960) Compiled by Ludwig Lauerhass,
Jr. ₍research assistant₎ Los Angeles, 1962.

x, 78 p. 22 cm.

Card
493

University of Kansas. Museum of Art.
Nineteenth century houses in Lawrence, Kansas; ₍exhibi-
tion₎ September 22–October 27, 1968. ₍Lawrence, Kan.,
1968₎

1 v. (unpaged) illus, maps. 23 cm. (*Its* Miscellaneous publications, no. 72)

Card
494

University of Rochester. *East Asian Library.*
Catalog of the East Asian collection, East Asian Library,
East Asian Language and Area Center, University of Ro-
chester. Rochester, N. Y., 1968.

592 p. 29 cm.

A list of the library's holdings in the Chinese and Japanese languages cataloged through May 1968, arranged by subject and author.

Card
495

University of Texas at Austin.
A catalogue of the Joanna Southcott collection at the
University of Texas, compiled by Eugene Patrick Wright.
₍Austin, Humanities Research Center₎ University of Texas
at Austin; ₍distributed by University of Texas Press, 1969,
c1968₎

138 p. illus. 26 cm. ₍Tower bibliographical series, 7₎ 7.50

1. Southcott, Joanna, 1750–1814—Bibliography.　　ɪ. Wright,
Eugene Patrick, 1936–　　ɪɪ. Title.　₍Series)

Z8828.4.T46　　　　016.1339′0924　　　68–65505
　　　　　　　　　　　　　　　　　　　　MARC

Library of Congress　　　₍2₎

Card
496

ANONYMOUS WORKS

There are many anonymous works of literary and historical renown such as epics, sagas, folk tales, religious writings and other works which have appeared under various names and titles, both in the original and in translations. Some of these classic and traditional works of unknown authorship are called "anonymous classics". In order to place the various editions and versions of the same anonymous work into a single group, each work is assigned a "uniform title" and this is used as the main entry. Each of these fifty representative works is listed under its assigned "uniform title" followed by a brief description of its contents.

1. Anglo-Saxon chronicle
   Chronological narrative of English history from the Roman invasion in 55 B.C. until 1154 A.D.
2. Arabian nights
   Collection of ancient Persian tales written in Arabic. Also known as <u>Thousand and one nights</u>.
3. Arthur, King
   Medieval romances based on a 6th century hero. Earliest manuscripts date from about the 12th century.
4. Aucassin et Nicolette
   Medieval French love story in prose and verse. Dates from the 12th century.
5. Avesta
   Zoroastrian scriptures of ancient Persia. Dates from about the 6th century B.C.
6. Beowulf
   Anglo-Saxon epic poem from the 8th century.
7. Bible
   Sacred scriptures of Christians.
8. Book of Mormon
   Sacred scriptures of the Mormon Church. First published in 1830.
9. Book of the Dead
   Collection of Egyptian funerary and religious texts. Dates from about the 6th century B.C.
10. Brahmanas
    Prose treatises explaining the significance of the Vedas. Dates from about 800-500 B.C.

11. Chanson de Roland
    French epic poem of the 11th century.
    Also known as <u>Song of Roland</u>.
12. El Cid Campeador
    Spanish epic poem of the 12th century.
13. Cinderella
    Traditional fairy tale of which the earliest
    known version dates from the 9th century in
    China.
14. Cuchulain
    Ancient Irish cycle of stories relating to
    the mythological hero, Cu Chulainn.
15. Dead Sea scrolls
    Various scroll manuscripts containing parts
    of the Old Testament and other religious
    writings in Hebrew and Aramaic dating from
    ca. 100 B.C. to 135 A.D. Found in caves
    near the coast of the Dead Sea in the late
    1940s and the 1950s.
16. Digby plays
    Medieval English religious plays.
17. Domesday book
    Census or survey of all lands in England.
    Completed in 1086 under orders of
    William the Conqueror.
18. Edda Saemundar
    Collection of Norse mythological poems dating
    from the 9th through the 13th centuries.
19. Eulenspiegel
    Medieval tales about the exploits of Tyll
    Eulenspiegel (i.e. Owlglass) and date from
    the 15th century.
20. Everyman
    Late 15th century morality play in English.
21. Exeter book
    Collection of Anglo-Saxon poetry compiled
    during the 10th century.
22. The Federalist
    Collection of 85 political essays by Alexander
    Hamilton, James Madison and John Jay. Published
    in 1788. Also known as <u>The Federalist papers</u>.
23. Gammer Gurton's needle
    Second oldest extant English comedy. First
    acted in 1566 at Cambridge and appeared in
    print in 1575.
24. Gesta Romanorum
    Medieval collection of popular tales in Latin
    in which each tale is characterized by a moral.
    First printed in Utrecht in 1472. Translated
    into English as <u>The Acts of the Romans</u>.

25. Goody Two Shoes
    English nursery tale of the 18th century.
26. Guillaume d'Orange
    Collection of medieval French epic poems
    of the 12th century.
27. Jatakas
    Tales and fables purporting to relate events
    in the lives of the Buddha when he was on his
    way to enlightenment. They date from about
    the 3rd century B.C.
28. Kalevala
    Finnish national epic composed of folk verses
    based on ancient poems of mythology. First
    published in present form in 1835.
29. Koran
    Sacred book of the Mohammedans dating from
    the 7th century.
30. Kormaks saga
    Icelandic love tale of the 13th century.
31. Lancelot
    French prose romance of the 13th century.
    Related to the King Arthur legends.
32. Legend of Kawelo
    Hawaiian folk tale.
33. Little Red Riding Hood
    Traditional folk tale. First published in
    France in 1697.
34. Mabinogion
    Collection of medieval Welsh stories and
    mainly relating to the Arthurian romances.
35. Mahabharata
    Sanskrit epic of ancient India, portions
    of which date from the 4th century B.C.
36. Merlin
    French prose romance of the 13th century.
    An early history of King Arthur.
37. Mother Goose
    Collection of nursery rhymes based on
    folklore and old wives' tales. First
    published in English in the 18th century.
38. Nibelungenlied
    Middle High German epic composed in the
    12th century. Also known as Song of the
    Nibelungs.
39. Njala
    Greatest of the Icelandic sagas and one of
    the latest. Dates from the 13th century.
    Also known as Njal's saga.

40. Oberammergau passion-play
    Passion play presented every 10 years at
    the Bavarian village of Oberammergau.
    First produced in 1634.
41. Reynard the Fox
    Medieval animal fable which satirizes
    contemporary life and events in Germany.
42. Robin Hood
    English ballads about a legendary outlaw
    of the 13th century.
43. Seven sages
    A cycle of stories of ancient oriental
    origin now appearing in various versions.
    Also known as <u>Seven wise masters of Rome</u>.
44. Stabat Mater
    Medieval Latin hymn on the Crucifixion.
    Probably written in the 13th century.
45. Talmud
    Jewish civil and religious law not contained
    in, but derived from the Pentateuch.
    "Talmud" used alone refers to the Babylonian
    Talmud which dates from the 5th century.
46. Talmud Yerushalmi
    Palestinian or Jerusalem Talmud. A smaller
    version which was completed a century
    earlier than the Babylonian Talmud.
47. Tripitaka
    Sacred writings of the Buddhists, parts of
    which date back to the 6th century B.C.
    Translated into English as <u>Three baskets</u>.
48. Upanishads
    Collection of Hindu treatises of the 6th
    century B.C. on the nature of man and the
    universe. Forms part of the Vedic writings.
49. Vedas
    Hindu scriptures of which the four chief
    books are the Rig-Veda, the Sama-Veda,
    the Atharva-Veda and the Yajur-Veda.
    They date from about 1500-1200 B.C.
    Also known as <u>Veda</u>.
50. Volsunga saga
    Icelandic prose saga assembled in the
    12th or 13th century. A Scandinavian
    prose version of the <u>Nibelungenlied</u>.

APPENDIX II

A LIST OF HEADINGS FOR UNITED STATES GOVERNMENT BODIES
DETERMINED ACCORDING TO THE
ANGLO-AMERICAN CATALOGING RULES   (NORTH AMERICAN TEXT)

This list of 300 headings of U.S. government agencies and bodies is exemplary rather than exhaustive; it is complete only insofar as there was an effort made to include at least one example of each type of agency. Every agency listed has been studied as to its organization, functions, purpose, and its relation to the government; then the appropriate Anglo-American rule was applied and the correct form of its name for cataloging purposes was determined.

The arrangement of Part I is alphabetical according to the form that would be used as a heading in the catalog. Following each entry is the number of the AA rule which was used to determine the correct form for that particular entry.

Part II is a list of the Anglo-American rules used and the numbers of the entries listed in Part I that contain headings which were determined by that specific rule.

These headings were all established according to the North American text of the Anglo-American cataloging rules. This includes the additions and changes approved by the A.L.A. Division of Cataloging and Classification and by the Library of Congress which were published in the Cataloging Service Bulletin #81 (September, 1967) of the Library of Congress Processing Department.

PART I -- Alphabetical List

U. S. Government Agencies	Anglo-American Cataloging Rule Number

1. Alaska Railroad. . . . . .78-A, type 6
2. American Battle Monuments Commission . . . . .78-A, type 1
3. American Printing House for the Blind. . . . . .78-A, type 6
4. Ames Research Center .78-A, type 2
5. Argonne Cancer Research Hospital . . . . .78-A, type 2
6. Argonne National Laboratory. . . . . .78-A, type 2
7. Armed Forces Staff College . . . . .78-A, type 2
8. Army Language School .78-A, type 2
9. Atomic Energy Commission . . . . .78-A, type 1
10. Atomic Energy Commission. Atomic Energy Laboratory. . . . .69, type 5
11. Bettis Atomic Power Laboratory . . . . .78-A, type 2
12. Bonneville Power Administration. . . . . .78-A, type 5
13. Brookhaven National Laboratory . . . . .78-A, type 2
14. Canal Zone 75
15. Civil Aeronautics Board. . . . . .78-A, type 5
16. Civil War Centennial Commission. . . . . .78-A, type 1
17. Clearinghouse for Federal Scientific and
     Technical Information . . . . .78-A, type 1
18. Coast and Geodetic Survey. . . . . .78-A, type 1
19. Command and Staff College. . . . . .78-A, type 2
20. Commission of Fine Arts. . . . . .78-A, type 1
21. Commodity Credit Corporation . . . . .78-A, type 6
22. Commodity Exchange Authority . . . . .78-A, type 5
23. Defense Documentation Center . . . . .78-A, type 2
24. Defense Electric Power Administration. . . . . .78-A, type 5
25. Delaware River Basin Commission. . . . . .78-A, type 4
26. District of Columbia .74-C
27. Export-Import Bank of Washington . . . . .78-A, type 6
28. Federal Communications Commission. . . . . .78-A, type 5
29. Federal Crop Insurance Corporation . . . . .78-A, type 6
30. Federal Deposit Insurance Corporation. . . . . .78-A, type 6
31. Federal Electric Corporation . . . . .78-A, type 6
32. Federal Facilities Corporation . . . . .78-A, type 6
33. Federal Home Loan Bank Board . . . . .78-A, type 6
34. Federal Maritime Commission. . . . . .78-A, type 5
35. Federal National Mortgage Association. . . . . .78-A, type 6
36. Federal Power Commission . . . . .78-A, type 5
37. Federal Prison Industries, Inc. . . . . .78-A, type 6
38. Federal Radiation Council. . . . . .78-A, type 1
39. Federal Reserve Bank of Atlanta. . . . . .78-A, type 6
40. Federal Reserve Bank of San Francisco. . . . . .78-A, type 6
41. Federal Reserve System . . . . .78-A, type 6
42. Federal Reserve System. Board of Governors. . . . . .69, type 1
43. Federal Savings and Loan Insurance Corporation . . . . . . .78-A, type 6
44. Federal-State Frost Warning Service. . . . . .78-A, type 4
45. Federal Theatre Project. . . . . .78-A, type 1
46. Federal Trade Commission . . . . .78-A, type 5
47. Federal Writers' Project . . . . .78-A, type 1
48. Fort Monroe. . . . . .78-A, type 3
49. Freer Gallery of Art .78-A, type 2
50. Gallaudet College. . . . . .78-A, type 2

U. S. Government Agencies

51.	Geological Survey.	.78-A, type 1
52.	George C. Marshall Space Flight Center	.78-A, type 2
53.	Goddard Space Flight Center.	.78-A, type 3
54.	Government Printing Office	.78-A, type 6
55.	Howard University.	.78-A, type 2
56.	Indian Arts and Crafts Board	.78-A, type 1
57.	Industrial College of the Armed Forces	.78-A, type 2
58.	Institute of Tropical Forestry	.78-A, type 1
59.	Interstate Commerce Commission	.78-A, type 5
60.	James Connally Air Force Base.	.78-A, type 3
61.	Job Corps.	.78-A, type 1
62.	John F. Kennedy Center for the Performing Arts	.78-A, type 2
63.	John F. Kennedy Space Center	.78-A, type 2
64.	Joint A.E.C.-N.A.S.A. Space Nuclear Propulsion Office.	.71-B
65.	Joseph H. Hirshhorn Museum and Sculpture Garden.	.78-A, type 2
66.	Knolls Atomic Power Laboratory	.78-A, type 2
67.	Langley Research Center.	.78-A, type 2
68.	Lawrence (E.O.) Radiation Laboratory	.67-A
69.	Lewis Research Center.	.78-A, type 2
70.	Library of Congress.	.78-A, type 2
71.	Lindsey Air Station.	.78-A, type 3
72.	Los Alamos Scientific Laboratory	.78-A, type 2
73.	Manned Spacecraft Center	.78-A, type 3
74.	Mound Laboratory	.78-A, type 2
75.	Mount Laguna Air Force Station	.78-A, type 3
76.	National Academy of Engineering.	.78-A, type 1
77.	National Academy of Sciences	.78-A, type 1
78.	National Air and Space Museum.	.78-A, type 2
79.	National Agricultural Library.	.78-A, type 2
80.	National Archives.	.78-A, type 2
81.	National Bureau of Standards	.78-A, type 1
82.	National Capital Housing Authority	.78-A, type 5
83.	National Capital Planning Commission	.78-A, type 1
84.	National Capital Regional Planning	.78-A, type 1
85.	National Center for Atmospheric Research	.78-A, type 2
86.	National Center for Health Statistics.	.78-A, type 2
87.	National Center for the Prevention and Control of Alcoholism	78-A, type 2
88.	National Collection of Fine Arts ;	.78-A, type 1
89.	National Commission of Food Marketing.	.78-A, type 1
90.	National Environmental Satellite Center.	.78-A, type 1
91.	National Foundation on the Arts and the Humanities	.78-A, type 1
92.	National Gallery of Art.	.78-A, type 2
93.	National Institute of General Medical Sciences	.78-A, type 2
94.	National Institute of Neurological Diseases and Blindness.	.78-A, type 2
95.	National Institute of Mental Health.	.78-A, type 2
96.	National Library of Medicine	.78-A, type 2
97.	National Museum.	.65-B
98.	National Office of Vital Statistics.	.78-A, type 1
99.	National Portrait Gallery.	.65-B
100.	National Reactor Testing Station	.78-A, type 2

	Anglo-American
U. S. Government Agencies	Cataloging Rule Number

101. National Referral Center for Science and Technology . . . .78-A, type 1
102. National Research Council . . . . .78-A, type 1
103. National Science Foundation . . . . .78-A, type 1
104. National Science Foundation. Office of Science
        Information Service. . . . . .69, type 2
105. National Transporation Safety Board . . . . .78-A, type 5
106. National War College. . . . . .78-A, type 2
107. National Zoological Park. . . . . : .78-A, type 3
108. Naval Biological Laboratory . . . . .78-A, type 2
109. Naval Dental School . . . . .78-A, type 2
110. Naval Observatory .78-A, type 2
111. Naval Photographic Center . . . . .78-A, type 2
112. Naval Postgraduate School . . . . .78-A, type 2
113. Naval Training Device Center. . . . . .78-A, type 2
114. Naval War College .78-A, type 2
115. Nevada Test Site. .78-A, type 3
116. Northern Rocky Mountain Forest and Range Experiment Station.78-A,type 2
117. Oak Ridge National Laboratory . . . . .78-A, type 2
118. Pacific Northwest Forest and Range Experiment Station . . .78-A, type 2
119. Panama Canal Company. . . . . .78-A, type 6
120. Peace Corps . . . . .78-A, type 1
121. Postal Savings System . . . . .78-A, type 6
122. Randolph Air Force Base . . . . .78-A, type 3
123. Red Cross (U.S.). .63-B and 65-B
124. Saint Elizabeths Hospital. . . . . .78-A, type 2
125. Sandia Laboratory .78-A, type 2
126. Saint Lawrence Seaway Development Corporation . . . . . . .78-A, type 6
127. Scott Air Force Base. . . . . .78-A, type 3
128. Securities and Exchange Commission. . . . . .78-A, type 5
129. Smithsonian Institution . . . . .78-A, type 2
130. Smithsonian Institution. Astrophysical Observatory . . . .78-A, type 2
131. Smithsonian Institution. Museum of History and Technology.78-A, type 2
132. Smithsonian Institution. Museum of Natural History . . . .78-A, type 2
133. Smithsonian Institution. Radiation Biology Laboratory. . .69, type 5
134. Smithsonian Tropical Research Institute . . . . .78-A, type 2
135. Southeastern Power Administration . . . . .78-A, type 5
136. Southwestern Power Administration . . . . .78-A, type 5
137. Tennessee Valley Authority. . . . . .78-A, type 5
138. U.S. Administration on Aging. 78-B
139. U.S. Agency for International Development 78-B
140. U.S. Agricultural Research Service. . . . . .78-A, type 1, exception
141. U.S. Agricultural Stabilization and Conservation Service. .78-A, type 1, exception
142. U.S. Air Force. 84
143. U.S. Architect of the Capitol 80-D
144. U.S. Armed Services Board of Contract Appeals 78-B
145. U.S. Arms Control and Disarmament Agency. 78-B
146. U.S. Army 84
147. U.S. Army Map Service 84
148. U.S. Army Medical Service 84
149. U.S. Board on Geographic Names. 78-B
150. U.S. Bureau of Agricultural Economics . . . . .78-A, Exception 1

	U. S. Government Agencies	Anglo-American Cataloging Rule Number

151. U.S. Bureau of American Ethnology . . . . .78-A, Exception 1
152. U.S. Bureau of Apprenticeship and Training. . . . . . .78-A, Exception 1
153. U.S. Bureau of Customs. 78-B
154. U.S. Bureau of Employment Security. 78-B
155. U.S. Bureau of Family Services. 78-B
156. U.S. Bureau of Federal Credit Unions. 78-B
157. U.S. Bureau of Fisheries. 78-B
158. U.S. Bureau of Indian Affairs 78-B
159. U.S. Bureau of Insular Affairs. 78-B
160. U.S. Bureau of Labor Standards. 78-B
161. U.S. Bureau of Land Management. 78-B
162. U.S. Bureau of Medicine and Surgery . . . . .78-A, Exception 1
163. U.S. Bureau of Mines. . . . . .78-A, Exception 1
164. U.S. Bureau of Naval Personnel. 78-B
165. U.S. Bureau of Outdoor Recreation 78-B
166. U.S. Bureau of Prisons. 78-B
167. U.S. Bureau of Public Roads 78-B
168. U.S. Bureau of Reclamation. . . . . .78-A, Exception 1
169. U.S. Bureau of Ships. . . . . .78-A, Exception 1
170. U.S. Bureau of the Budget 78-B
171. U.S. Bureau of the Census 78-B
172. U.S. Bureau of the Mint 78-B
173. U.S. Business and Defense Services Administration . . .78-A, type 1, exception
174. U.S. Central Intelligence Agency. 78-B
175. U.S. Children's Bureau. 78-B
176. U.S. Civil Service Commission 78-B
177. U.S. Civil Rights Commission. 78-B
178. U.S. Coast Guard. 84
179. U.S. Community Relations Service. 78-B
180. U.S. Congress 78-B
181. U.S. Congress. House 81-A
182. U.S. Congress. Senate. 81-A
183. U.S. Consulate, Medellin. 85
184. U.S. Consumer and Marketing Service . . . . .78-A, type 1, exception
185. U.S. Copyright Office 78-B
186. U.S. Council of Economic Advisers 78-B
187. U.S. Court of Appeals (2d Circuit). 83-C
188. U.S. Defense Atomic Support Agency. . . . . .78-A, type 1, exception
189. U.S. Defense Communications Agency. 78-B
190. U.S. Defense Contract Audit Agency. 78-B
191. U.S. Defense Intelligence Agency. 78-B
192. U.S. Defense Supply Agency. 78-B
193. U.S. Dept. of Agriculture . . . . .78-A, Exception 1
194. U.S. Dept. of Agriculture. Economic Research Service .78-A, Exception 2
195. U.S. Dept. of Agriculture. Graduate School . . . . . .78-A, Exception 2
196. U.S. Dept. of Commerce. . . . . .78-A, Exception 1
197. U.S. Dept. of Defense . . . . .78-A, Exception 1
198. U.S. Dept. of Health, Education, and Welfare. . . . . .78-A, Exception 1
199. U.S. Dept.of Housing and Urban Development. . . . . . .78-A, Exception 1
200. U.S. Dept. of Justice . . . . .78-A, Exception 1

U.S. Government Agencies

201.	U.S. Dept. of Labor	78-A, Exception 1
202.	U.S. Dept. of Labor. Office of Manpower, Automation and Training	78-A, Exception 2
203.	U.S. Dept. of State	78-A, Exception 1
204.	U.S. Dept. of the Interior.	78-A, Exception 1
205.	U.S. Dept. of Transportation.	78-A, Exception 1
206.	U.S. District Court (Delaware).	83-C
207.	U.S. Division of Water Supply and Pollution Control	78-A, Exception 1
208.	U.S. Economic Development Administration.	78-B
209.	U.S. Embassy (Colombia)	85
210.	U.S. Environmental Science Services Administration.	78-A, type 1, exception
211.	U.S. Executive Office of the President.	78-B
212.	U.S. Farm Credit Administration	78-A, type 1, exception
213.	U.S. Farmer Cooperative Service	78-A, type 1, exception
214.	U.S. Farmers' Home Administration	78-A, type 1, exception
215.	U.S. Federal Aviation Administration.	78-A, type 1, exception
216.	U.S. Federal Bureau of Investigation.	78-B
217.	U.S. Federal Coal Mine Safety Board of Review	78-B
218.	U.S. Federal Committee on Pest Control.	78-B
219.	U.S. Federal Extension Service.	78-B
220.	U.S. Federal Highway Administration	78-A, type 1, exception
221.	U.S. Federal Housing Administration	78-B
222.	U.S. Federal Mediation and Conciliation Service	78-B
223.	U.S. Federal Railroad Administration.	78-A, type 1, exception
224.	U.S. Federal Water Pollution Control Administration	78-A, type 1, exception
225.	U.S. Fish and Wildlife Service.	78-A, type 1, exception
226.	U.S. Food and Drug Administration	78-B
227.	U.S. Foreign Agricultural Service	78-A, type 1, exception
228.	U.S. Foreign Broadcast Information Service.	78-A, type 1, exception
229.	U.S. Foreign Claims Settlement Commission	78-B
230.	U.S. Forest Service	78-A, type 1, exception
231.	U.S. General Accounting Office.	78-B
232.	U.S. General Services Administration.	78-B
233.	U.S. Housing and Home Finance Agency.	78-B
234.	U.S. Immigration and Naturalization Service	78-B
235.	U.S. Information Agency	78-B
236.	U.S. Internal Revenue Service	78-B
237.	U.S. Legation (Bulgaria).	85
238.	U.S. Manpower Administration.	78-A, type 1, exception
239.	U.S. Marine Corps	84
240.	U.S. Maritime Administration.	78-A, type 1, exception
241.	U.S. Military Sea Transportation Service.	78-B
242.	U.S. Mission to the United Nations.	86
243.	U.S. Narcotics Bureau	78-B
244.	U.S. National Aeronautics and Space Administration.	78-A, type 1, exception
245.	U.S. National Labor Relations Board	78-B
246.	U.S. National Mediation Board	78-B
247.	U.S. National Park Service.	78-A, type 1, exception
248.	U.S. National Railroad Adjustment Board	78-B
249.	U.S. National Security Agency	78-B
250.	U.S. National Security Council.	78-B

U. S. Government Agencies

251.	U.S. Naval Air Systems Command	.84
252.	U.S. Naval Air Transport Service	.84
253.	U.S. Navy	.84
254.	U.S. Office of Coal Research	.78-A, Exception 1
255.	U.S. Office of Economic Opportunity	.78-B
256.	U.S. Office of Education	.78-A, Exception 1
257.	U.S. Office of Emergency Planning	.78-B
258.	U.S. Office of Naval Operations	.78-B
259.	U.S. Oil Import Administration	.78-B
260.	U.S. Operations Mission to Ecuador	.86
261.	U.S. Patent Office	.78-B
262.	U.S. Post Office Dept.	.78-A, Exception 1
263.	U.S. President	.80-A
264.	U.S. President's Appalachian Regional Commission	.78-B
265.	U.S. President's Committee on Equal Employment Opportunity	.78-B
266.	U.S. Public Health Service	.78-A, type 1, exception
267.	U.S. Railroad Retirement Board	.78-B
268.	U.S. Renegotiation Board	.78-B
269.	U.S. Rural Community Development Service	.78-B
270.	U.S. Rural Electrification Administration	.78-B
271.	U.S. Secret Service	.78-B
272.	U.S. Selective Service System	.78-B
273.	U.S. Small Business Administration	.78-A, type 1, exception
274.	U.S. Social Security Administration	.78-B
275.	U.S. Soil Conservation Service	.78-A, type 1, exception
276.	U.S. Subversive Activities Control Board	.78-B
277.	U.S. Supreme Court	.83-A
278.	U.S. Tariff Commission	.78-B
279.	U.S. Tax Court	.83-A
280.	U.S. Technical Cooperation Mission to India	.86
281.	U.S. Trade Mission to Brazil	.86
282.	U.S. Treasury Dept.	.78-A, Exception 1
283.	U.S. Veterans Administration	.78-B
284.	U.S. Vocational Rehabilitation Administration	.78-A, type 1, exception
285.	U.S. Wage and Hour and Public Contracts Divisions	.78-A, Exception 1
286.	U.S. Weather Bureau	.78-A, Exception 1
287.	U.S. Welfare Administration	.78-B
288.	U.S. White House Office	.78-B
289.	U.S. Women's Bureau	.78-A, Exception 1
290.	United States Botanic Garden	.78-A, type 1
291.	United States Coast Guard Academy	.78-A, type 2
292.	United States Military Academy	.78-A, type 2
293.	United States Naval Academy	.78-A, type 2
294.	United States Travel Service	.78-A, type 1
295.	Veterans Administration Center, Wichita	.78-A, type 2
296.	Veterans Administration Hospital, Ann Arbor	.78-A, type 2
297.	Volunteers in Service to America	.78-A, type 1
298.	Wallops Station	.78-A, type 3
299.	Walter Reed Army Medical Center	.78-A, type 2
300.	Yosemite National Park	.78-A, type 3

PART II -- Index

APPENDIX III

A LIST OF HEADINGS FOR GOVERNMENTAL BODIES
OF GREAT BRITAIN AS DETERMINED BY THE
BRITISH NATIONAL BIBLIOGRAPHY
ACCORDING TO THE
ANGLO-AMERICAN CATALOGUING RULES (BRITISH TEXT)

The following list of 200 British government
agencies and bodies are those used by the British National
Bibliography and determined according to the British text
of the Anglo-American cataloguing rules.

Included in this consolidated list are many of the
most commonly used names of British governmental bodies and
agencies. The hierarchy is often shown to give the cataloger the full name of the body which will serve as an aid
and a guide in determining the correct name of similar
bodies which are not listed here.

A comparison of the names in this list with those
in Appendix II will bring out the variations due to the
use of the two different texts of the Anglo-American cataloging rules.

1. Advisory Committee on Drug Dependence. Hallucinogens
        Sub-Committee.
2. Advisory Council on the Penal System.
        (Hierarchy: Great Britain. Home Office. Advisory
                    Council on the Penal System.)
3. Advisory Panel on Problems Arising From the Use of
        Asbestos.
        (Hierarchy: Great Britain. Factory Inspectorate.
                    Advisory Panel on Problems Arising From
                    the Use of Asbestos.)
4. Advisory Panel on Students Maintenance Grants.
        (Hierarchy: Great Britain. Scottish Education
                    Department. Advisory Panel on Students
                    Maintenance Grants.)
5. Aeronautical Research Council.
        (Hierarchy: Great Britain. Ministry of Technology.
                    Aeronautical Research Council.)
6. Agricultural Research Council.
7. Air Registration Board.
8. Air Transport Licensing Board.
        (Hierarchy: Great Britain. Board of Trade. Air
                    Transport Licensing Board.)

9. Anti-Locust Research Centre.
   (Hierarchy: Great Britain. Ministry of Overseas
               Development. Anti-Locust Research
               Centre.)
10. Bank of England.
11. British Broadcasting Corporation.
12. Building Research Station.
   (Hierarchy: Great Britain. Ministry of Public
               Buildings & Works. Building Research
               Station.)
13. Carpet Industry and Training Board.
14. Central Advisory Council for Education (Wales).
   (Hierarchy: Great Britain. Department of Educa-
               tion & Science. Central Advisory
               Council for Education (Wales).
15. Central Committee on English.
16. Central Health Services Council.
   (Hierarchy: Great Britain. Department of Health
               & Social Security. Central Health
               Services Council.)
17. Central Training Council.
   (Hierarchy: Great Britain. Ministry of Labour.
               Central Training Council.)
18. Central Youth Employment Executive.
   (Hierarchy: Great Britain. Ministry of Labour.
               Central Youth Employment Executive.)
19. Church of England. Liturgical Commission.
20. Church of England. Liturgy and ritual.
21. Committee for the Diploma in Management Studies.
22. Committee of Enquiry on Pressure Vessels.
   (Hierarchy: Great Britain. Ministry of Technology.
               Committee of Enquiry on Pressure Vessel
23. Committee of Scientists on the Scientific & Technolog-
    ical Aspects of the Torrey Canyon Disaster.
24. Committee on Bird Sanctuaries in the Royal Parks (Englan
    & Wales)
   (Hierarchy: Great Britain. Ministry of Public
               Building & Works. Committee on Bird
               Sanctuaries in the Royal Parks
               (England & Wales).
25. Committee on General Practice.
26. Committee on Herbage Seed Supplies.
   (Hierarchy: Great Britain. Home Office. Committee
               on Herbage Seed Supplies.)
27. Committee on Hospital Scientific & Technical Services.
   (Hierarchy: Great Britain. Department of Health &
               Social Security. Committee on Hospital
               Scientific & Technical Services.)
28. Committee on Research & Development in Modern Languages
29. Committee on the Management of Local Government.
30. Committee on the More Effective Use of Technical Colleg
    Resources.
   (Hierarchy: Great Britain. Department of Education
               & Science. National Advisory Council c
               Education for Industry & Commerce.
               Committee on the More Effective Use of
               Technical College Resources.)

31. Committee on Tribology.
    (Hierarchy: Great Britain. Ministry of Technology.
                Committee on Tribology.)
32. Council for Scientific Policy.
33. Council on Tribunals.
34. Countryside Commission.
35. Decimal Currency Board.
36. Engineering Industry Training Board.
37. Falkland Islands Dependencies Survey.
38. Food Standards Committee.
    (Hierarchy: Great Britain. Ministry of Agriculture,
                Fisheries, and Food. Food Standards
                Committee.)
39. Footpaths Committee.
40. Forest Products Research Laboratory.
    (Hierarchy: Great Britain. Ministry of Technology.
                Forest Products Research Laboratory.)
41. Forestry Commission.
42. Great Britain.
    (Hierarchy: Great Britain. Ministry of Defence.
                Admiralty Board.)
43. Great Britain. Army.
44. Great Britain. Board of Inland Revenue.
45. Great Britain. Board of Trade.
46. Great Britain. Census Office.
47. Great Britain. Central Office of Information.
48. Great Britain. Central Statistical Office.
49. Great Britain. Charity Commission.
50. Great Britain. Civil Service Commission.
51. Great Britain. Commission for Inquiring into the Em-
    ployment & Condition of Children in Mines and
    Manufactories.
52. Great Britain. Court of Chancery.
53. Great Britain. Court of Chancery. Petty Bag Office.
54. Great Britain. Crown Estate Commissioners.
55. Great Britain. Customs & Excise.
56. Great Britain. Department of Agriculture & Fisheries
    for Scotland.
57. Great Britain. Department of Education & Science.
58. Great Britain. Department of Education & Science.
    Committee on Football.
59. Great Britain. Department of Employment & Productivity.
60. Great Britain. Department of Health & Social Security.
61. Great Britain. Directorate of Overseas Surveys.
    (Hierarchy: Great Britain. Ministry of Overseas
                Development. Directorate of Overseas
                Surveys.)
62. Great Britain. Exchequer & Audit Department.
63. Great Britain. Factories Inquiry Commission.
64. Great Britain. Factory Inspectorate.
    (Hierarchy: Great Britain. Ministry of Labour.
                Factory Inspectorate.
65. Great Britain. Foreign and Commonwealth Office.
66. Great Britain. Foreign Compensation Commission.

67. Great Britain. General Board of Health.
68. Great Britain. General Post Office.
69. Great Britain. General Register & Record Office of
    Shipping & Seamen.
        (Hierarchy: Great Britain. Ministry of Transport.
                    General Register & Record Office of
                    Shipping & Seamen.)
70. Great Britain. General Register Office.
71. Great Britain. General Register Office. Advisory
    Committee on Medical Nomenclature & Statistics.
    Sub-Committee on Classification of Mental Disorders.
72. Great Britain. General Register Office, Scotland.
73. Great Britain. General Register Office of Births,
    Deaths, & Marriages, Scotland.
74. Great Britain. Government Social Survey Department.
75. Great Britain. Her Majesty's Stationery Office.
76. Great Britain. High Court of Admiralty.
77. Great Britain. High Court of Justice.
        (Hierarchy: Great Britain. Supreme Court of Judi-
                    cation. High Court of Justice.)
78. Great Britain. Home Office.
79. Great Britain. Home Office. Departmental Committee
    on Criminal Statistics.
80. Great Britain. Home Office. Fire Department.
81. Great Britain. Hydrographic Department.
        (Hierarchy: Great Britain. Navy Department. Hydo-
                    graphic Department.)
82. Great Britain. Industrial Assurance Commissioner.
83. Great Britain. Inspector of Explosives.
        (Hierarchy: Great Britain. Home Office. Inspector
                    of Explosives.)
84. Great Britain. Land Registry.
85. Great Britain. Laws, statutes, etc.
86. Great Britain. Mines Inspectorate.
        (Hierarchy: Great Britain. Ministry of Power.
                    Mines Inspectorate.)
87. Great Britain. Ministry of Agriculture, Fisheries &
    Food.
88. Great Britain. Ministry of Defence.
89. Great Britain. Ministry of Housing & Local Government.
90. Great Britain. Ministry of Labour.
91. Great Britain. Ministry of Labour. Manpower Research Unit.
92. Great Britain. Ministry of Overseas Development.
93. Great Britain. Ministry of Power.
94. Great Britain. Ministry of Public Building & Works.
95. Great Britain. Ministry of Public Building & Works.
    Directorate of Building Management.
96. Great Britain. Ministry of Technology.
97. Great Britain. Ministry of Transport.
98. Great Britain. Monopolies Commission.
99. Great Britain. Navy Department.
100. Great Britain. Navy Department. Navigation & Direction
    Division.

101. Great Britain. Parliament.
102. Great Britain. Parliament. House of Commons.
103. Great Britain. Parliament. House of Commons. Committee
     on Employment of Boys in Sweeping of Chimnies.
104. Great Britain. Parliament. House of Commons. Select
     Committee on Lunatics.
105. Great Britain. Parliament. House of Commons. Select
     Committee on Silver & Gold Wares.
106. Great Britain. Parliament. House of Lords.
107. Great Britain. Parliament. House of Lords. Select
     Committee on Colonization from Ireland.
108. Great Britain. Parliament. House of Lords. Select
     Committee on the African Slave Trade.
109. Great Britain. Parliament. Select Committee on
     Artisans & Machinery.
110. Great Britain. Parliament. Select Committee on Public
     Libraries.
111. Great Britain. Parliamentary Commissioner for
     Administration.
112. Great Britain. Poor Law Commission.
113. Great Britain. Prison Department.
114. Great Britain. Privy Council.
115. Great Britain. Public Schools Commission.
116. Great Britain. Registry of Friendly Societies.
117. Great Britain. Royal Air Force.
118. Great Britain. Royal Commission on Local Government
     in England.
119. Great Britain. Royal Commission on Local Government
     in Scotland.
120. Great Britain. Royal Commission on Medical Education.
121. Great Britain. Royal Commission on Trade Unions and
     Employers' Associations.
122. Great Britain. Royal Navy. Naval Intelligence Division.
123. Great Britain. Royal Navy. Supply & Transport Service.
124. Great Britain. Scottish Development Department.
125. Great Britain. Scottish Education Department.
126. Great Britain. Scottish Home & Health Department.
127. Great Britain. Scottish Land Court.
128. Great Britain. Scottish Office.
129. Great Britain. Scottish Office. Regional Development
     Division.
130. Great Britain. Supplementary Benefits Commission.
          (Hierarchy: Great Britain. Department of Health
                       & Social Security. Supplementary
                       Benefits Commission.)
131. Great Britain. Transport Tribunal.
132. Great Britain. Treasury.
133. Great Britain. Treasury. Management Accounting Unit.
134. Great Britain. Trustee Savings Banks Inspection
     Committee.
          (Hierarchy: Great Britain. Treasury. Trustee
                       Savings Banks Inspection Committee.)
135. Great Britain. Welsh Office.

136. Historic Buildings Council for Scotland.
137. Historical Manuscripts Commission.
138. Hydraulics Research Station.
      (Hierarchy: Great Britain. Ministry of Technology.
            Hydraulics Research Station.)
139. India Office Library.
140. Industrial Safety Advisory Council.
      (Hierarchy: Great Britain. Ministry of Labour.
            Industrial Safety Advisory Council.)
141. Inter-Service Metallurgical Research Council.
      (Hierarchy: Great Britain. Ministry of Technology.
            Inter-Service Metallurgical Research
            Council.)
142. Joint Fire Research Organisation.
      (Hierarchy: Great Britain. Ministry of Technology.
            Joint Fire Research Organisation.
143. Joint Standing Committee on Safety in the Use of Power
     Presses.
144. Laboratory of the Government Chemist.
      (Hierarchy: Great Britain. Ministry of Technology.
            Laboratory of the Government Chemist.)
145. Land Commission.
146. Law Commission.
      (Hierarchy: Great Britain. Lord Chancellor's
            Department. Law Commission.)
147. Law Reform Committee.
      (Hierarchy: Great Britain. Lord Chancellor's Office.
            Law Reform Committee.)
148. Library Advisory Council (England)
      (Hierarchy: Great Britain. Department of Education
            & Science. Library Advisory Council
            (England).
149. Management Study Team on Development Control.
150. Medical Research Council.
151. Meteorological Office.
      (Hierarchy: Great Britain. Ministry of Defence.
            Meteorological Office.)
152. National Advisory Council on Education for Industry &
     Commerce.
      (Hierarchy: Great Britain. Department of Education
            & Science. National Advisory Council
            on Education for Industry & Commerce.)
153. National Agricultural Advisory Service.
      (Hierarchy: Great Britain. Ministry of Agriculture,
            Fisheries & Food. National Agricultural
            Advisory Service.)
154. National Air Traffic Control Service.
      (Hierarchy: Great Britain. Board of Trade. National
            Air Traffic Control Service.)
155. National Board for Prices & Incomes.
156. National Committee for Commonwealth Immigrants.
157. National Computing Centre.
158. National Economic Development Council.

159. National Engineering Laboratory.
   (Hierarchy: Great Britain. Ministry of Technology.
        National Engineering Laboratory.)
160. National Environment Research Council.
161. National Food Survey Committee.
   (Hierarchy: Great Britain. Ministry of Agriculture,
        Fisheries & Food. National Food
        Survey Committee.)
162. National Lending Library for Science & Technology.
   (Hierarchy: Great Britain. Department of Education
        & Science. National Lending Library
        for Science & Technology.)
163. National Parks Commission.
164. National Research Development Corporation.
165. National Savings Committee.
166. National Youth Employment Council.
   (Hierarchy: Great Britain. Department of Employment
        & Productivity. National Youth Employ-
        ment Council.)
167. Natural Environment Research Council.
168. Nautical Almanac Office.
   (Hierarchy: Great Britain. Navy Department.
        Nautical Alamanc Office.)
169. North West Planning Council.
   (Hierarchy: Great Britain. Department of Economic
        Affairs. North West Planning Council.)
170. Open University Planning Committee.
   (Hierarchy: Great Britain. Department of Education
        & Science. Open University Planning
        Committee.)
171. Ordnance Survey.
   (Hierarchy: Great Britain. Ministry of Agriculture,
        Fisheries & Food. Ordnance Survey.)
172. Patent Office.
173. Police Advisory Board for Scotland.
174. Public Health Laboratory Service Board.
175. Public Record Office.
176. Public Works Loan Board.
177. Red Deer Commission.
178. Review Body on Doctors' & Dentists' Remuneration.
179. Road Research Laboratory.
   (Hierarchy: Great Britain. Ministry of Transport.
        Road Research Laboratory.)
180. Royal Aircraft Establishment, Farnborough.
181. Royal Commission on the Ancient & Historical Monuments
   & Constructions of England.
182. Royal Mint.
   (Hierarchy: Great Britain. Treasury. Royal Mint.)
183. Schools Council.
   (Hierarchy: Great Britain. Department of Education
        & Science. Schools Council.)
184. Scottish Certificate of Education Examination Board.
185. Scottish Health Services Council.
186. Scottish Record Office.

187. Scottish Valuation Advisory Council.
        (Hierarchy: Great Britain. Scottish Development
                    Department. Scottish Valuation Ad-
                    visory Council.)
188. Social Science Research Council.
189. Sports Council.
        (Hierarchy: Great Britain. Department of Educa-
                    tion & Science. Sports Council.)
190. Standing Commission on Museums & Galleries.
191. Torry Research Station.
        (Hierarchy: Great Britain. Ministry of Technology.
                    Torry Research Station.)
192. Tribunal Appointed to Inquire into the Disaster at
        Aberfan on October 21st, 1966.
193. Tropical Products Institute.
        (Hierarchy: Great Britain. Ministry of Overseas
                    Development. Tropical Products Institute.)
194. University Grants Committee.
        (Hierarchy: Great Britain. Department of Educa-
                    tion & Science. University Grants
                    Committee.)
195. Warren Spring Laboratory.
        (Hierarchy: Great Britain. Ministry of Technology.
                    Warren Spring Laboratory.)
196. Water Resources Board.
197. Water Supply Industry Training Board.
198. Working Group on Manpower for Scientific Growth.
        (Hierarchy: Great Britain. Ministry of Technology.
                    Working Group on Manpower for Scientific
                    Growth.)
199. Working Party on Scales of Provision.
        (Hierarchy: Great Britain. Department of Education
                    & Science. Sports Council. Working
                    Party on Scales of Provision.)
200. Yorkshire & Humberside Economic Planning Council & Board.
        (Hierarchy: Great Britain. Department of Economic
                    Affairs. Yorkshire & Humberside
                    Economic Planning Council & Board.)

REFERENCES

American Library Association. Division of Cataloging and Classification. _A.L.A. cataloging rules for author and title entries_. 2d ed. Edited by Clara Beetle. Chicago, 1949.

Anglo-American cataloging rules. Prepared by the American Library Association, the Library of Congress, the Library Association and the Canadian Library Association. North American text. Chicago, American Library Association, 1967.

Anglo-American cataloguing rules. Prepared by the American Library Association, the Library of Congress, the Library Association and the Canadian Library Association. British text. London, Library Association, 1967.

Cataloging service bulletin. (Library of Congress. Processing Department.) Bulletins 79-83, January 1967 - September 1968.

Catalogue & index; periodical of the Library Association Cataloguing and Indexing Group. Numbers 6 - 16, April 1967 - October 1969.

Colloquium on the Anglo-American Cataloging Rules, University of Toronto, 1967. _The code and the cataloguer_; proceedings of the Colloquium on the Anglo-American Cataloging Rules, held at the School of Library Science, University of Toronto on March 31 and April 1, 1967. Edited by Katherine H. Packer and Delores Phillips. Supervising editor: Katherine L. Ball. Toronto, University of Toronto Press, 1969.

Gorman, Michael. _A study of the rules for entry and heading in the Anglo-American cataloguing rules, 1967 (British text)_. London, Library Association, 1968.

Hines, Theodore C. "Anglo-American cataloging rules." (Review of the North American text.) _College & Research Libraries_, v. 29, no. 1, January 1968. p. 62-3

New rules for an old game; proceedings of a workshop on the 1967 Anglo-American cataloguing code held by the School of Librarianship, the University of British Columbia, April 13 and 14, 1967. Edited by Thelma E. Allen [and] Daryl Ann Dickman. Vancouver, University of British Columbia, 1967.

Osborn, Andrew D.   "AA cataloging code."   (Review and comparison of the North American text and the British text.)   _Library Journal_, v. 93, no. 17, October 1, 1968. p. 3523-25.

Seminar on the Anglo-American Cataloguing Rules (1967), University of Nottingham, 1968.   _Proceedings of the Seminar_ organized by the Cataloguing and Indexing Group of the Library Association at the University of Nottingham, 22nd-25th March 1968.   Edited by J. C. Downing and N. F. Sharp.   London, Library Association, 1969.

INDEX

References are to page numbers